MW00966183

Our
Greatest
Treasure

Our Greatest Treasure

Cy Mersereau

OUR GREATEST TREASURE, PART ONE
Copyright © 2017 by Cy Mersereau

All rights reserved. Neither this publication nor any part of this publication may be reproduced or transmitted in any form or by any means, electronic or mechanical, including photocopying, recording or any information storage and retrieval system, without permission in writing from the author.

Scripture quotations marked (KJV) are taken from the Holy Bible, King James Version, which is in the public domain. Scripture quotations marked (NKJV) taken from the New King James Version®. Copyright © 1982 by Thomas Nelson. Used by permission. All rights reserved. Scripture quotations marked (NLT) are taken from the Holy Bible, New Living Translation, copyright ©1996, 2004, 2007, 2013 by Tyndale House Foundation. Used by permission of Tyndale House Publishers, Inc., Carol Stream, Illinois 60188. All rights reserved. Scripture quotations marked (NASB) taken from the New American Standard Bible®, Copyright © 1960, 1962, 1963, 1968, 1971, 1972, 1973, 1975, 1977, 1995 by The Lockman Foundation. Used by permission. Scripture quotations are from the ESV® Bible (The Holy Bible, English Standard Version®), copyright © 2001 by Crossway, a publishing ministry of Good News Publishers. Used by permission. All rights reserved. Scripture quotations marked HCSB are taken from the Holman Christian Standard Bible®, Copyright © 1999, 2000, 2002, 2003, 2009 by Holman Bible Publishers. Used by permission. Holman Christian Standard Bible®, Holman CSB®, and HCSB® are federally registered trademarks of Holman Bible Publishers.

Printed in Canada

ISBN: 978-1-4866-0198-1

Word Alive Press
131 Cordite Road, Winnipeg, MB R3W 1S1
www.wordalivepress.ca

MIX
Paper from
responsible sources
FSC
www.fsc.org   FSC® C016245

Library and Archives Canada Cataloguing in Publication

Mersereau, Cyril E., 1947-, author
     Our greatest treasure / Cy Mersereau.

Issued in print and electronic formats.
ISBN 978-1-4866-1049-5 (paperback).--ISBN 978-1-4866-1050-1 (pdf).--
ISBN 978-1-4866-1051-8 (html).--ISBN 978-1-4866-1052-5 (epub)

     1. Bible. Old Testament--Criticism, interpretation, etc. I. Title.

BS1171.3.M47 2016   221.6   C2015-908736-8
                                          C2015-908737-6

"Your word is a lamp to my feet and a light to my path."
—Psalm 119:105, NKJV

Of the Incomparable Treasure of the Holy Scriptures,
with a Prayer for the True Use of the Same

Here is the spring where waters flow, to
quench our heart of sin:
(Isa. 12:3 and 49:10; Rom. 5:16 and 6:17)
Here is the tree where truth doth grow; to lead our lives therein:
(Jer. 33:15 and Ps. 119:160)
Here is the judge that stints the strife, when men's devices fail:
(Rev. 2:7 and 22:2; Ps. 119:142,144)
Here is the bread that feeds the life, that death cannot assail.
(John 6:35)
The tidings of salvation dear, comes to our ears from hence:
(Luke 2:10)
The fortress of our faith is here, and shield of our defense.
(Eph. 6:16)
Then be not like the hog that hath a pearl at his desire,
(Matt. 7:6)
And takes more pleasure in the trough and wallowing in the mire.
(2 Pet. 2:22)
Read not this book in any case, but with a single eye:
(Matt. 6:22)
Read not but first desire God's grace to understand thereby.
(Ps. 119:27,73)
Pray still in faith with this respect, to fructify therein,
(Jude 20)
That knowledge may bring this effect, to mortify thy sin.
(Ps. 119:11)
Then happy thou in all thy life, what so to thee befalls.
(Josh. 1:8)
Yea, double happy shalt thou be, when God by death thee calls.
(Ps.1:1, 2;94:12,13)[1]

---

[1] *Geneva Bible* (White Hall, WV: Tolle Leg Press, 2006—1007), Preface. Originally written in 1599.

DEDICATION

It is with deep gratitude that this book is dedicated to Elisabeth Owen, who so patiently and efficiently laboured through all of my original material. She transferred all of such to her computer and assumed the task of initial editing. Elisabeth is named for her namesake in Luke 1:41, taken from the King James Version of the Scriptures. She is the only daughter of John and Lisa Owen, and sister to three younger brothers. She lives in Truro, Nova Scotia. From our first acquaintance, this wonderful family has warmly embraced me and encouraged me in every way. Elisabeth is a born-again believer who is deeply committed to the Lord's service. She is a graduate of New Brunswick Bible Institute at Victoria Corner, New Brunswick.

ACKNOWLEDGEMENTS

I am deeply indebted to a strong cast of individuals who have played a large part in the making of this book. The wonderful people at Wesley United Church in Hunts Point, Nova Scotia, have been a rock of love and support. Jerry and Judy Kane, along with their sons Jay and Jason, pray for me regularly and often welcome me to their home, listening patiently as I talk incessantly about my most recent writing project. It is always such a blessing to visit with them. Carman and Marg Mason have kindly opened their home to me, giving me a place of privacy to write when I am on the road. Carman is a walking concordance who can always find the verse of Scripture that has somehow eluded me. I value their friendship.

The enclosed was formerly part of a much more extensive manuscript, which was largely completed by Elisabeth Owen with some touch-up from Jennifer Lyons and Jamie Goyetche. The material needed major revision before being submitted for publication, and this task was completed by Bonnie Carter. She made needed changes, coordinated the citations, and reformatted chapter divisions. The final format is her doing and she is to be commended for a job well done.

Thanks again to all of the wonderful people at Word Alive Press for their kind attention to detail and professional approach throughout the process. They are truly writer-friendly, giving valuable suggestions to enable us to get a quality product to the public.

All praise to our Heavenly Father, who invites us to walk on holy ground every time we access His blessed Word. I am so thankful for that time many years ago when I really heard His Word with understanding for the very first time, resulting in my conversion. Glory to God, who sent the Son to be the Saviour of the world (1 John 4:14).

Thy Word Is Truth

Truth is fidelity to a given standard, and according to the Scriptures, absolute truth is embodied in the Lord Jesus Christ and embedded in the words of Scripture (John 14:6; 17:17). The Word of God gives instruction for living meaningful and worthwhile lives (Psalm 119:105) and instills joy in our hearts as we avail ourselves of its precious truths. The psalmist expresses well his sheer delight in God's precepts in Psalm 119:162: *"I rejoice in your word like one who discovers a great treasure"* (NLT).

The Bible needs no validation from outside sources, but it will soon become apparent that in terms of history, geography, chronology, and archaeology, the Scriptures prove to be fully accurate and consistently reliable at every turn. This volume will present a sustained argument that the Word of God is exactly what it says it is and can be safely trusted in every detail. A part of this writing will also focus on a few individuals whose lives have been fully transformed by the message of the Bible. They are representative of the many millions of humankind who have been forever changed by the power of God's Word.

Our greatest treasure is the Word of God. The words of Scripture should be our sustenance, our meditation, our authority, and our delight. Every doctrine, every teaching, every movement, every denomination, every religion, every motive, every utterance, and every experience must be measured against the backdrop of

Holy Writ. We can be set free from all that is fleshly, false, and fraudulent as we garner the eternal truths that are inherent in Scripture. Jesus said, *"And ye shall know the truth, and the truth shall make you free"* (John 8:32, KJV). People who know the Scriptures will be far less likely to be tempted, swayed, or enslaved by the vain and vacuous sects and cults that are rife in our society.

The Bible, comprised of the Old and New Testaments, encompasses the sacred writings of the Christian faith. The bedrock of all truth is found in the Scriptures, and that truth is settled in heaven (Psalm 119:89). Many of the teachings of Holy Writ are clear and uncompromising. They are not up for grabs. Even so, our culture is determined to pressure believers into adopting standards and philosophies that are clearly contrary to the Scriptures. When we cannot be persuaded to abandon truth, we are pummelled with slander, name-calling, and even legal action. The Christian life is far from a cakewalk; it is a daily challenge that will test us in every way imaginable.

Taking a journey into the Bible is both exciting and challenging. We never know what we are going to find. Some of us may be forced to come to grips with teachings that are contrary to what we have been taught by our culture, our schools, our parents, or even by our church. We will also find that, while some doctrines are well-defined and agreed upon by Christians from a variety of backgrounds and denominations, other issues have often spawned debates, divisions, and diatribes among God's people. There is perhaps no other arena where Christian virtue is so severely tested than that which entails differences between believers. I will venture to say that some of us have used up far more time and energy to try to bring a fellow Christian to our particular viewpoint than we have ever exercised to bring a non-believer to Christ.

I am unreservedly and unabashedly committed to the truth of Scripture. There are things in the Bible I do not fully understand, things I find difficult to accept, and things that annoy me, but that does not in any way negate the truth of what is there. There are things that excite me, encourage me, and give me hope and assurance, and it is all God's truth.

Your Bible, which may have remained unopened for far too long, is indeed your greatest treasure. Open it up and mine its precious truths. Allow the Holy Spirit to drive its blessed truths home to your heart.

Thy words were found, and I did eat them; and thy word was unto me the joy and rejoicing of mine heart: for I am called by thy name, O Lord God of hosts. (Jeremiah 15:16, KJV)

Mark Buchanan campaigns for the entire Bible:

The book—God-breathed, every word of it—is useful. Useful for what? For propping up overheads? No. For studying the ancient languages and customs and cultures of the Middle East? Well, maybe. But that's not what Paul had in mind. How about for devising and defending certain theological systems? Again, we're wandering off the mark. The Bible is useful for this: shaping and training you to be the kind of person who walks in righteousness and is ready to do good works—God's works in a fallen world. If you are not using the Word of God for that, you're misusing it.[2]

Buchanan then goes on to say that we often run from the Scripture because of the God we meet there, who is not anything like we have ever imagined. Buchanan stands convinced that we need to read and study *all* of the Bible, not just the passages that appeal to us. None of it should be ignored, because God wants us to have all of it with nothing excepted.

There's so much in the Bible that bores us—those Levitical laws on mold and goats, the endless genealogies in 1 Chronicles; there's so much that puzzles us—God ambushing Moses, bent on murder until Zipporah circumcises her son and touches the bloody foreskin to Moses' feet; there's so much that frightens us—all those brutal wars, God ordering the death of women and children, or making the earth open wide to swallow families whole. And what about this God who hardens Pharaoh's heart and then punishes him for it, who anoints Saul king and then repents of it? Who loves David, and then goes on to describe, in almost more detail than we can digest, his maimings, his murders, his wife-stealing… Maybe we like our Bibles softened, sharpened, explained, embellished, tidied up, boiled down. Both distilled and diluted. David ruddy-cheeked and virtuous, groomed for Sunday school, a portrait of Middle America vigour and piety. Ezekiel 23, the prophet's shockingly graphic depiction of Judah and Israel as two adulterous sisters, censored out. Judges' concubine cut into twelve pieces and mailed to the tribes bowdlerized [purged of graphic and gory details]. Narratives and parables whittled down to principles. Stark commands dressed up as funny anecdotes.

---

[2] Mark Buchanan, *Your God Is Too Safe: Experiencing the Wonder of a God You Can't Control* (Colorado Springs, CO: Multnomah, 2001), 202.

Speak to us yourself and we will listen. But do not have God speak to us.[3]

The Bible has been treated too casually by too many Christians for far too long. It needs to be read often, and it needs to be read in its entirety. It should not be accessed for just our favourite passages or to satisfy the requirements of a daily devotional guide. All of its wonders and mysteries need to be explored repeatedly and consistently.

We need to take quality time to study the portions that are difficult and unpleasant—yes, even those boring and often laborious chapters filled with names and more names. The fact of the matter is that those passages comprise a very small percentage of biblical content, but the Holy Spirit placed them there for our profit and instruction. For instance, one of the more incredible facts to be discovered in the genealogies is that women occupy a significant place in the line of Christ, while in countless pagan cultures women have no recognition in the family tree. Many of the men and women listed are mentioned only once in all of Scripture, but some are accompanied by significant personal details that give them a special place in the history of God's outworking in the human race.

There are horror stories in the Bible which remind us of the utter depravity of the human race because of the fall of humanity described in Genesis. Resist the temptation to skip those terrible acts of violence, including the massacre of women and children and other frightful atrocities. We cringe as we witness the unarmed Agag being mercilessly cut down by Samuel, but generations earlier the Amalekites had, without provocation, attacked the Israelites as they made their long and difficult trek from Egypt to the Promised Land (1 Samuel 15:32–35).

We gasp in horror at the deception and intrigue employed by the left-handed Ehud in order to find entry into the private quarters of Eglon, king of the Moabites, whereupon the obese monarch was dispatched with a knife buried deep in his abdomen. This single act of warfare allowed the nation of Israel to enjoy eighty years of peace free from further harassment by their Moabitish cousins (Judges 3:12–30). Nearly two chapters are devoted to Jephthah, the son of a prostitute, who became an outstanding judge in Israel. We are left breathless as Jephthah, on the eve of battle, promises to offer up the first living thing to leave his front door as a sacrifice in the event of victory. His subsequent success only increases the suspense and raw emotion as he arrives home to be greeted by his only child, a young daughter. Hollywood has never come close to matching

[3] Ibid., 203–204.

such a crescendo of raw human emotion and intensity of mounting suspense—and to top it off, it's all true!

But don't forget the pleasantries, especially the story of Joseph in Genesis 37–50, which gives us perhaps the most perfect "type" of Christ in the whole Bible.

Now these things happened to them as an example, but they were written down for our instruction, on whom the end of the ages has come. (1 Corinthians 10:11, ESV)

Read the book of Ruth in one sitting and allow yourself to relish God's wondrous plan of redemption, beautifully illustrated by Ruth and Boaz.

Having a bad day? Read the psalms and allow their truths to soothe your soul and calm your nerves.

Have a few questions about life that seem void of an answer? So does the book of Job! In fact, there are over three hundred questions in this forty-two-chapter book.

Allow yourself to walk for a while in the shoes of Jeremiah, who prophesied and wept over Jerusalem for over forty years. Read how unpopular he was and how he desperately wanted to vacate the ministry but found it impossible to do so. He said that God's *"word was in mine heart as a burning fire shut up in my bones, and I was weary with forbearing, and I could not stay"* (Jeremiah 20:9, KJV).

The one great truth to which I tenaciously adhere is that the only means of salvation available to any people in any era of history is grace. Every human being that ever was saved before Moses, during the time of Moses, or after Moses was saved by grace through faith alone. From the time of Abel (Hebrews 11:4) to the present day, all who are redeemed come by way of the cross, the juncture of human history, where the saints of both testaments converge, coalesce, congeal, and continue as one body on into eternity. This surely is the teaching of Ephesians 2:12–18. Verse 14 says, *"For he is our peace, who hath made both one, and hath broken down the middle wall of partition between us"* (KJV). The impression given by some that God is somehow a harsh and unbending tyrant in the Old Testament who suddenly morphs into a loving and gentle Sovereign in the New Testament is both false and misleading.

Aiden Wilson Tozer puts this into proper perspective:

The spring of Christian morality is the love of Christ, not the law of Moses; nevertheless there has been no abrogation of the principles of morality contained in the law. No privileged class exists exempt from that righteousness which the law enjoins...

The Old Testament is indeed a book of law, but not of law only. Before the great flood Noah "found grace in the eyes of the Lord," and after the law was given God said to Moses, "Thou hast found grace in my sight." [Genesis 6:8 and Exodus 33:12]...

Had the Old Testament times been times of stern, unbending law alone the whole complexion of the early world would have been vastly less cheerful than we find it to be in the ancient writings. There could have been no Abraham, friend of God; no David, man after God's own heart; no Samuel, no Isaiah, no Daniel. The eleventh chapter of Hebrews, that Westminster Abbey of the spiritually great of the Old Testament, would stand dark and tenantless. Grace made sainthood possible in Old Testament days just as it does today.

No one was ever saved other than by grace, from Abel to the present moment. Since mankind was banished from the east-ward Garden, none has ever returned to the divine favor except through the sheer goodness of God. And wherever grace found any man [or woman] it was always by Jesus Christ. Grace indeed came by Jesus Christ, but it did not wait for His birth in the manger or His death on the cross before it became operative.

Christ is the Lamb slain from the foundation of the world. The first man in human history to be reinstated in the fellowship of God came through faith in Christ. In olden times men looked forward to Christ's redeeming work; in later times they gaze back upon it, but always they came and they come by grace, through faith.[4]

---

[4] A.W. Tozer, *The Knowledge of the Holy* (New York, NY: Harper One, 1961), 94–95.

CHAPTER ONE

Understanding of the Times

For the word of God is quick, and powerful, and sharper than any twoedged sword, piercing even to the dividing asunder of soul and spirit, and of the joints and marrow, and is a discerner of the thoughts and intents of the heart. (Hebrews 4:12, KJV)

For to one is given by the Spirit the word of wisdom; to another the word of knowledge by the same Spirit... to another discerning of spirits... (1 Corinthians 12:8,10, KJV)

A PASTORAL PERSPECTIVE

It was my happy privilege, on a trip to Chipman, New Brunswick in 2008, to visit with a man who had garnered the respect of numerous families and individuals through more than sixty years of gospel ministry. Earlier that same year, several months shy of his ninety-first birthday, the Rev. Harry Branscombe decided to retire.

Harry's former home is located on the lower end of Maple Street, just down the hill from where my maternal grandparents used to live. In my boyhood days, I would spend time with Harry's younger son during my summer visits to Chipman.

Catching up on the news of our respective families, we reflected on the challenge of ministry in today's turbulent society. Harry's comments are worthy of note, especially seen against the backdrop of his many years of pastoral ministry.

Fully confirming my deepest suspicions, this long-serving minister of the gospel observed that Bible-reading and Bible study are on a noticeable decline among Christians today. He further offered that the Old Testament is especially ignored, considered by many to be unnecessary and irrelevant in our postmodern society.[5]

Why are we finding such an evident lack of interest in God's Word along with spiritual decline among God's people? Harry suggested that the very real difficulty lies with the pulpit ministry in our churches. He was convinced that too many pastors with a comfortable salary and attractive benefits are more sensitive to the feelings of their people than being faithful to the Word of God. Facing private and public censure and possible loss of position, preachers too often sacrifice biblical truth on the altar of present convenience.

Taking this a step further, Harry stated that many Christians spend too much time reading books *about* the Bible rather than spending quality time reading the Bible itself. He believed that God's people should prioritize their time to maximize more opportunities to read the Bible. Harry passed away on December 28, 2011, at the age of ninety-four.

Woodrow Kroll has stated, "The Bible is the best-loved and never-read book of all time."[6] It cannot be denied that the book displayed on our coffee tables, carried down the aisle by brides, used in courts of law to administer oaths, given as an award at graduation, and deposited in the back of our church pews, is now a treasured but neglected object. The Word of God is not valued in the same way as with former generations and is not esteemed as with some who were tortured and killed for reading it publicly or translating it into the language of the people. Kroll gives his assessment:

> I do think it's well past time we stopped spending so much on church buildings and start spending more on building the church. The church needs revival. But every great revival in the Bible was accompanied by, if not initiated by the rediscovery of God's Word...More than anything,

---

[5] Harry had already read the entire Old Testament twice since the beginning of the year when I visited him in early July.

[6] Woodrow Kroll, *Back to the Bible: Turning Your Life Around with God's Word* (Sisters, OR: Multnomah, 2000), 15.

the church of the twenty-first century needs to fall in love again with the word of God.[7]

NAMES AND MORE NAMES

Perhaps no other book of the Bible has received such negative press as 1 Chronicles. With its massive genealogies, it is considered by many to be a Bible reader's ultimate nightmare; we just cannot seem to get past all those names!

Of the twenty-nine chapters that make up the historical account, a full fifteen chapters are devoted to preserving for posterity the names of hundreds of people. The Jewish people of today find richness and purpose as God's covenant nation, noting that God has reserved both the names and professions of their ancestors.

The first nine chapters give us a detailed, tightly knit genealogical accounting that takes us from Adam to the Babylonian captivity. The writer acquaints us with the most important men and women in the history of Israel.[8] The eleventh chapter introduces us to the list of David's mighty men (1 Chronicles 11:10). Following the death of Saul and his sons in 1 Chronicles 10:1–6, David gathers his forces to Hebron (1 Chronicles 12:23–40), strengthening his grip on the leadership of Israel. Along with the massive numbers of military personnel enumerated here, Israel's new king inherited the services of two hundred men of superior intelligence from the tribe of Issachar. We shall soon see that their leadership skills would prove invaluable to both David and the nation of Israel. 1 Chronicles 23–25 comprise the division of the Levites and the names of musicians.

1 Chronicles 26 then records the divisions of the gatekeepers, the naming of the keepers of the treasure (by families), and those set aside for judicial duties in the outer areas of the nation. In 1 Chronicles 27, the writer details more prominent military officers and the chief officers of the tribes, as well as various overseers and counsellors.

Many question why God gives us so many names, so many numbers, and so many details so far removed from us today, but the more you read the Bible the more you realize the unity, correctness, and purpose of all that has been included in His inspired Word.

Let us take a closer look at what was going on during that period of Israel's history.

---

[7] Woodrow Kroll, *Taking Back the Good Book* (Wheaton, IL: Crossing Books, 2007), 88.

[8] One such example is Jabez and his beautiful prayer, popularized in recent years by Bruce Wilkinson in his *Prayer of Jabez*, and the sequel *Beyond Jabez* (see 1 Chronicles 4:9–10).

David's ascension to the throne finally brought Israel to full nationhood, which never transpired under the disjointed rule of Saul. David's plan for a temple in Jerusalem would centralize monotheistic worship of Jehovah and end the restlessness and disruption that was a part of tabernacle worship. David's insight and vision are given in 1 Chronicles 23, for he said,

> *The Lord God of Israel has given rest to His people, and He dwells in Jerusalem forever. Also, the Levites will no longer need to carry the tabernacle and all its utensils for its service.* (1 Chronicles 23:25–26, NASB)

It is obvious that the writer of 1 Chronicles has access to a wealth of well-documented information from which to formulate his meticulous account. Drawing heavily on the earlier accounts in Samuel and First and Second Kings, after recording his titanic genealogy, he records historical events at breathtaking speed. The fourteen verses of 1 Chronicles 10 recount the defeat and death of Saul and his sons, the Philistine defilement of Saul's body, the kindness of the people of Jabesh-Gilead in giving proper burial to the king and his sons, and a brief summary of Saul's sins, which answers why he lost his battle, his kingdom, and his life.

Following the death of Saul, David is installed as the king of Israel, and he immediately organizes his military personnel and sets out to consolidate his kingdom. For years, David had heard the taunts of the inhabitants of Jebus, thinking they were invincible behind their enormous walls. Supported by the vast majority of Israelites and surrounded by his mighty men, he captures the Jebusite stronghold and firmly establishes his capital in Jerusalem. Archaeologists have fully excavated the water tunnel (2 Samuel 5:8) by which David and his men, using ropes, pulleys, grappling hooks, and ladders, found access to the heavily guarded fortress. Not only did he capture the city, he renamed it, expanded its environs, and made it the centre of Jewish worship (2 Samuel 5:6–10).

According to historians, the city of Jerusalem, also called Zion, "had been besieged, captured, or destroyed in whole or in part more than forty times."[9] Here Solomon would build the first Jewish temple. This temple was destroyed by the Babylonians, but later on, under the decree of Cyrus, a second temple was built under the direction of Zerubbabel.[10]

---

[9] G. Frederick Owen, "Archaeological Supplement," s.v. "Jerusalem," in *The Thompson Chain-Reference Bible*, ed. Frank Charles Thompson (Indianapolis, IN: B.B. Kirkbride, 1988), 1759.
[10] See the book of Ezra for details.

The second temple never came close to the glory of Solomon's grand enterprise, and by 63 B.C., when Pompey captured the city with his Roman army, it lay largely in ruin. In 19 B.C., a major restoration of Zerubbabel's temple began under the direction of Herod the Great, and it was not completed until 64 A.D. This partially constructed temple, known as Herod's temple, is the one referred to in the New Testament and which was destroyed by Roman legions only six years after its completion.

A VITAL CONNECTION

Nearly one thousand years after David's time, into Herod's temple comes a Visitor who, in a few short years, would not only be the talk of the town but the talk of the world. He stayed behind after His parents left the city, and in the temple He was surrounded by some of the more learned and scholarly Jewish teachers of the day.

Astonished and amazed at the knowledge and spiritual insight of this twelve-year-old boy, they could not know that this descendant of King David was the promised Messiah (Luke 2:42–52). More than two decades later, this same Jesus, the son of Mary and Joseph (as was supposed), who had ministered publicly for over three years, was condemned by the Jewish authorities and turned over to Roman officials for public humiliation and execution. Having been taken outside the ancient fortification of the Jebusites and beyond the walls of the city of Jerusalem, He was taken to a hill (Mark 15:22–27) where, along with two criminals, He was nailed to a cross.

Returning to 1 Chronicles, we find that the entire twelfth chapter is a throwback to a time before 11:1–47 and summarizes the narrative covered in 1 Samuel 27 to 2 Samuel 5. A common anomaly of Hebrew script is to add further details after the fact. Nestled deep in this passage is the verse that gives rise to the title for this chapter:

And of the children of Issachar, which were men that had understanding of the times, to know what Israel ought to do; the heads of them were two hundred; and all their brethren were at their commandment. (1 Chronicles 12:32, KJV)

From Jewish sources,[11] including the Talmud, we learn that the descendants of Issachar, Leah's fifth son with Jacob, were among the most educated and

---

[11] *New Bible Dictionary* (Downers Grove, IL: Intervarsity Press, 2007), 532.

intelligent in all of Israel. No less than two hundred of them were prominent leaders, and their influence spread beyond their own tribe to the remainder of Israel.

The word *understanding* in the verse above combines two Hebrew words into one, giving it a richness of meaning that is not readily apparent when translated into English. The word has reference to insight, discernment, and wisdom, usually referring to wisdom that responds to God and His Word. It also includes the ability to teach and communicate that wisdom and knowledge to others so they can become aware of God's will in a given situation. Their natural giftedness and spiritual discernment were given to benefit all of Israel.

The New Testament equivalent is to be found in 1 Corinthians 12:1–12. The gifts mentioned in this passage are given to enhance the ministry of the whole body of Christ, not for the aggrandizement of a few. The two gifts that seem to have the closest proximity to the "understanding" of 1 Chronicles 12:32 are wisdom and discernment (1 Corinthians 12:8,10). No gift is more needed today than that of discernment, or, as some versions rightly translate, to "distinguish the spirits."[12] With so many belief systems calling for our attention, we need to know God's Word in order to discern the spirit of truth from the spirit of error (1 John 4:1–6).

The knowledgeable and discerning men from the tribe of Issachar knew God and understood the unfolding events taking place in the nation. This enabled them to be instructive to the other tribes. Never before in their history had the descendants of Abraham known such unity. Toward the end of this chapter we find in 1 Chronicles 12:38, where the emphasis is laid on *"all Israel"* and *"one mind"* to recognize the kingship of David.

With their chosen king established in Jerusalem, the real battle for national identity had begun. Both David and the nation had numerous sworn enemies, and their unity and loyalty would be severely tested in the days ahead. Surrounding nations, including the Philistines and the Syrians, continued to harass the Israelites. There were men of giant stature among the Philistines, relations of Goliath, who, like modern-day terrorists, were determined to kill David and destroy his kingdom. David's killing of Goliath made him a lightning rod for revenge, so much so that on at least one occasion his men forbade him to enter the theatre of battle.

The insightful leaders of the tribe of Issachar can teach us a great deal about coming to grips with the spirit of the age in which we live. Their loyalty to

---

[12] Check out 1 Corinthians 12:10 in the NASB or ESV.

their anointed king through troublesome times should be an inspiration to our generation today. Possibly the only Scriptures available to them were the first five books of the Old Testament (no more than eight), but they acted on what they knew. They fully understood, and so should we, that they were a chosen covenant people whom God would use to bless the world with the coming of Messiah. According to the Abrahamic Covenant in Genesis 12:1–3, God's agreement with Israel's famous ancestor had both physical and spiritual implications. With the agreement extending through David (1 Chronicles 17), the King of Israel is assured that his throne, through Solomon, will last forever.

The careful reader of God's Word will grasp the truth that there is far more here than an earthly kingdom progressing and prospering under the able leadership of an earthly king. Political and national ambitions are most certainly an ever-present reality, but through this militaristic and political process, the God of Abraham, Isaac, and Jacob was preparing the descendants of Abraham to be His vessel to bring the promised redemption to the world.

The people of Issachar had a grasp of the times in which they lived and also understood their place in history as God's covenant people. They were surrounded by enemies who hated their presence in the land God had promised them. The reign of Saul had left many of the Israelites disillusioned and desperate for stable leadership. Families and tribes were divided, caught between Saul's corrupt activities and David's accomplishments.

KNOWING OUR CULTURE

Our present culture lies in a virtual wasteland of relativism (the theory that all criteria and value judgments vary with individuals, circumstances, and cultures), pluralism (that one religious belief is as valid as another), subjectivism (that feelings and personal opinions are paramount to objective reality), and nihilism (that there is no basis for knowledge or truth). John MacArthur takes this to its logical conclusion, suggesting that, in the mindset of our culture, "we really cannot know anything with any degree of certainty."[13]

Undetected by many Christians in our evangelical churches, this abstract approach to truth has found its way into our worship services and Bible studies. We need not be surprised when, in the face of authoritative and objective teaching and preaching of God's Word, people are seen squirming in their seats because they have been duped into believing that we really cannot be certain about anything. According to contemporary intellectualism, the only absolute is

---

[13] John MacArthur, *The Truth War: Fighting for Certainty in an Age of Deception* (Nashville, TN: Thomas Nelson, 2007), 22.

that there are no absolutes, which is blatantly contrary to the Word of God we have neglected for far too long.

In an age of uncertainty and deception, there now rages in the church a battle for certainty. Our only source for truth is denied by the world and neglected by the church. The Bible is no longer read, studied, taught, or preached as it once was in former times. The people of Issachar in the days of David were able to discern their times and respond accordingly because they had the written Word of God from Moses and the spoken Word of God from Samuel. Their familiarity with God's sacred Word enabled them to give wise counsel and godly direction to the rest of the nation. 1 Chronicles 12:32 says that they *"understood the times, with knowledge of what Israel should do..."* (NASB)

The twentieth century produced more translations of the Bible in all languages than any other period in church history. The English language alone now boasts more than one thousand different kinds of Bibles, including scores of translations, paraphrases, and numerous study Bibles from a vast array of theological persuasions. In 2008, one prominent television evangelist offered his viewers three different study Bibles in a four-month timeframe. In the face of such sincere and well-intentioned efforts to promote the Bible, it still remains a fact that Bible-reading and Bible study are low on our priority list.

Some moral issues addressed in the Scriptures have in our day become politically charged, which makes the challenge even greater for Christians. Our culture prides itself on being inclusive and celebrates diversity. What this really means is that all unwanted opinions are excluded by means of name-calling, public humiliation, and negative press, with perhaps even a court appearance thrown in. Free speech has been granted to everybody except people who use the Bible as their basis for a standard of morality. Words like bigot, homophobic, insensitive, hateful, and intolerant are liberally applied to sincere Christians whose desire is to glorify God and uphold His Word. For instance, when the Word of God is proclaimed and placarded at a gay pride parade in England, it is seen as spreading hate literature.

A very recent instance reported by Cornerstone Gospel Ministries in California shows how far our culture has moved away from biblical truth:

Of course you recognize the title, "Silent Night." Likely you heard this hymn or sang it within the past few weeks. It was composed in Austria in the early 1800's and is a classic blend of lyrics and music. God must be praised for the talents of Joseph Mohr and Franz Gruber. Recently, a school in Kings Park, New York, used this hymn in their assembly for the winter concert. One of the parents attending was startled by the omission of every reference to the birth of Christ. Was this by design or just an accident? Since the choir rehearsed it in this manner for sometime, it was deliberate.

School district officials the school's principal and the choir director, basically passing the buck. Typical politics? Yes or no. The exception is that every word relative to Jesus Christ was removed. This is exclusionary and a prime example of contemporary efforts to not only diminish religion in the public sector—but put Christ to death a second time. For this, no Christian should be silent.[14]

---

[14] From an email message to the author. June 1, 2014.

CHAPTER TWO

Manipulation of the Mind

The Law of the Lord is perfect, reviving the soul; the testimony of the Lord is sure, making wise the simple; the precepts of the Lord are right, rejoicing the heart; the commandment of the Lord is pure, enlightening the eyes; the fear of the Lord is clean, enduring forever; the rules of the Lord are true, and righteous altogether. More to be desired are they than gold, even much fine gold; sweeter also than honey and drippings of the honeycomb. Moreover, by them is your servant warned; in keeping them there is great reward. (Psalm 19:7–11, ESV)

Conviction is strong and emotion runs deep through the 176 verses of Psalm 119. The Word of God is named or inferred in every verse of this powerful and persuasive portion of Holy Writ. In verse 97, the writer expresses his love for God's Word, and in verse 160 he utters his conviction that we can rely on God's Word. It is a helpful reality check to see if we show the psalmist's passion for the Word of God. Some questions we need to ask are as follows:

- Do we share David's love for God's Word, or are we indifferent to its claim on our lives?
- Are we committed to the reading of God's Word on a regular basis?

- Do we welcome opportunities to share God's truth with others?
- Have we endeavoured to view the social and moral issues of our time through the lens of God's Word?

The church is in danger of selling out to a generation of professing Christians who feel no loyalty to an authoritative Bible and desire no corrective preaching from the pulpit. Our culture has little interest in objective truth, having more concern for feelings and experience. We now face a major credibility crisis within the church, for we are fast becoming a church without a Bible. John MacArthur explains why we are in such a confused state:

> The clarity and sufficiency of Scripture, the lostness of unredeemed humanity, and the justice of God in condemning sinners are all long standing convictions in every major strain of historic Christianity. Christians have differed among themselves about peripheral questions or lesser points of doctrine. But historically and collectively Christians have always been in full agreement that whatever is true—whatever is objectively and ontologically true—is true whether any given individual understands it, likes it or receives it as truth. In other words, because reality is created and truth is defined by God, what is really true is true for everyone, regardless of anyone's personal perspective or individual preferences. These days, however, people are experimenting with subjective, relativistic ideas of truth and labeling them "Christian." This trend signals a significant departure from biblical and historic Christianity.[15]

Taking this a step further, MacArthur gives us the clincher:

> The true meaning of Scripture or anything else, for that matter—has already been determined and fixed by the mind of God.[16]

Rather than a straight-from-the-shoulder delivery of God's truth, which was standard procedure for past generations, we now hear words like sensitive, pliable, flexible, etc. being applied to our presentation of the gospel. "Thus saith the Lord" is now replaced with an interactive chat and a time of nonjudgmental sharing. The emergent church movement has grown ever stronger in recent

---

[15] MacArthur, *The Truth War*, xxii.
[16] Ibid., xxi.

years and is responsible for many long and heated discussions among God's people. Christian music is now described as either traditional, contemporary, or "emergent." I wonder if our churches will soon be differentiated in the same way.

The following quote from one of the influential leaders in the emergent church movement raises some degree of alarm:

> I don't think we've got the gospel right yet... I don't think the liberals have it right. But I don't think we have it right either. None of us has arrived at orthodoxy.[17]

Does this sound like the same gospel Paul preached and for which he was ultimately martyred in Rome? Is this the gospel that turned the world upside-down? (Acts 17:6) The same person, when asked about homosexuality, said we should wait five years before making a pronouncement on whether or not this sexual orientation is sinful.[18] Incredibly, this popular speaker, who was raised in a Christian environment, now suggests that adherents of non-Christian religious systems can go to heaven without faith and repentance (see 1 Timothy 4:1–5 and Jude 3–4).[19] The words of novelist Thomas Hardy are well worth some thought: "the serpent hisses where the sweet birds sing…"[20]

Over one hundred years ago, a businessman-turned-preacher by the name of D.L. Moody said words that, if repeated in any of our churches today, would ring as true as they were then:

> WHAT WE NEED TODAY IS MEN WHO BELIEVE IN THE BIBLE FROM THE CROWN OF THEIR HEADS TO THE SOLES OF THEIR FEET: WHO BELIEVE IN THE WHOLE OF IT, THE THINGS THEY UNDERSTAND, AND THE THINGS THEY DO NOT UNDERSTAND![21]

The very first chapter of David Marshall's excellent book, *The Truth Behind the New Atheism*, is entitled "Have Christians Lost their Minds?"[22] The last I

---

[17] Ibid., x.

[18] Ibid., 139.

[19] Brian D. McLaren, *A Generous Orthodoxy* (Grand Rapids, MI: Zondervan, 2004), 17, 293–295.

[20] Thomas Hardy, *Tess of the D'Urbervilles* (Mineola, NY: Dover Publications, Inc., 2001), 59–60.

[21] Harold Lindsell, *The Bible in the Balance* (Grand Rapids, MI: Zondervan, 1979), 27. On one occasion when Moody, surrounded by reporters, was asked to respond to a liberal preacher who insisted that the story of Jonah and the whale was a myth, he replied, "I stand by Jonah" (Ibid., 26).

[22] David Marshall, *The Truth Behind the New Atheism* (Eugene, OR: Harvest House, 2007), 15.

heard, we haven't, but our powers of reasoning are being seriously challenged and manipulated by a strong postmodern culture that has found its way into the church by way of the emergent church movement.

Before we move on, we must define our terms. Manipulation refers to a cleverly designed mechanism that is carefully and systematically disarming us and skillfully changing our thought patterns about the Bible. Instead of embracing without reservation the basic tenets of the Word of God, we now find ourselves questioning and scrutinizing every facet of our Christian faith. This all-pervading influence is commonly labelled postmodernism, but what does this term entail? This new and insidious way of thinking is defined by John MacArthur:

> Postmodernism in general is marked by a tendency to dismiss the *possibility* of any sure and settled knowledge of the truth. Postmodernism suggests that if objective truth exists, it cannot be known objectively or with any degree of certainty. That is because (according to postmodernists), the subjectivity of the human mind makes knowledge of objective truth impossible. So it is useless to think of truth in objective terms. Objectivity is an illusion. Nothing is certain, and the thoughtful person will never speak with too much conviction about anything. Strong convictions about any point of truth are judged supremely arrogant and hopelessly naïve. Everyone is entitled to his own truth.[23]

MacArthur then compresses this lengthy definition into a nutshell:

> It is the rejection of every expression of certainty... all this is ultimately a vain attempt to try to eliminate morality and guilt from human life.[24]

Christian orthodoxy is not built on a blind faith with nothing to give it foundational roots, as is often the charge from detractors such as Richard Dawkins. In his book *The Selfish Gene*, Dawkins accuses Christians of exercising a kind of faith that he defines as "a kind of mental illness... a state of mind that leads people to believe something—it doesn't matter what—in the total absence of supporting evidence."[25] The Bible believer needs only to look up into the heavens to witness an abundance of evidence for a Supreme Intellect and Master Designer who by His own inherent power holds the universe together

---

[23] MacArthur, *The Truth War*, 10–11.

[24] Ibid., 12–13.

[25] Marshall, *Truth Behind the New Atheism*, 16.

(Hebrews 11:1; Romans 1:20–21; Colossians 1:16–17). For us, it would indeed be absolute blindness to even entertain the thought that all of this came about by chance or accident.

David Wells gives us a clear picture of what transpires when God is no longer part of the equation:

> In a fallen world, Fate, Chance, Material, and Emptiness then assume God's place in life. They become the organizing forces in the creation. The outworking of this inner hollowness nevertheless appears to be the essence of wisdom (1 Cor. 3:20)! However the "more the unbroken man marches along this road secure of himself," wrote Barth, "the more surely does he make a fool of himself, the more certainly do that morality and that manner of life which are built up upon forgetting the abyss, upon a forgetting of men's true home, turn out to be a lie. The vanity, emptiness, and futility of fallen reason are the affliction visited upon sinners by God's judgement… What the postmodern world celebrates is its rejection of all absolutes and in its assumed right to define all reality privately is a sign of God's wrath (cf. Rom. 1:22).[26]

Christians need to be aware that the postmodern mindset has already deeply penetrated many of our evangelical churches, being carried along by the manipulative techniques of the emergent church. While our minds are being manipulated, our faith is being eroded by a movement that gives all the signs of being what church ought to be but is not even close to the New Testament pattern. Far more emphasis is given to culture than to Christ, and while being sensitive to our culture we are gradually being desensitized to the authority of the Bible.

An article entitled "The Emergent Kingdom" was featured in the January/ February 2010 issue of *Israel My Glory*. The opening sentences are alarming:

> The emergent church considers itself a conversation, not a movement. As such it is a loose coalition of Christian leaders welded together by a postmodern philosophy of ministry that rejects much of the theology evangelicals have held dear. There is little attempt to rally around doctrinal positions which are often seen as out-of-date in a pluralistic world.[27]

---

[26] David Wells in *The Supremacy of Christ in a Postmodern World*, ed. John Piper and Justin Taylor (Wheaton, IL: Crossway Books, 2007), 45. Copyright held by Desiring God Ministries.
[27] Gary E. Gilley, "The Emergent Kingdom," *Israel My Glory*, January/February 2010, 26–28.

According to this article, the emergents believe that "hell was invented by the Pharisees and that redemption from sin is not the real need of humanity."[28]

Emergent philosophy is very simply the revival of the gospel that was expressed by liberal and modernistic elements in the nineteenth and twentieth centuries. An inclusivistic theology assures all individuals that they are already part of the Kingdom of God.

Emergent Christians are persuaded that no issue relating to biblical theology is ever finally settled but must be constantly adapted to an ever changing culture.

> The central propositions and bedrock convictions of biblical Christianity—such as firm belief in the... authority of Scripture, a sound understanding of the true gospel, full assurance of salvation... the lordship of Christ, and the narrow exclusivity of Christ as the only way of salvation—do not reconcile well with postmodernism's contempt for clear, authoritative truth claims.[29]

---

[28] Ibid., 27.
[29] MacArthur, *The Truth War*, 18.

CHAPTER THREE

The Legacy of Richard John Uniacke

In 2008, I took the opportunity to visit the estate at Mount Uniacke, located on the old Windsor Road about forty kilometres from Halifax, Nova Scotia. At one time part of an eleven-thousand-acre estate, the area is much smaller now, but the crowning jewel was and still is the huge mansion which houses the original furniture from over two hundred years ago. Built in 1813 by Richard John Uniacke, the longest-serving Attorney General of Nova Scotia, the dwelling overlooks nearby Lake Martha, named for Uniacke's beloved first wife, Martha Maria.[30]

The life of Richard John Uniacke portrays how the Bible was seen by both the common people and the more prominent citizens of Nova Scotia over two hundred years ago. Uniacke looked upon the Bible as a sacred document, a treasure trove of truth entrusted to us by God. He embraced its teachings and taught them to his family. His philosophy was based on the Bible and could be seen in both his personal life and political policy.

Richard and Martha's marriage was an unlikely union, even by the standards of the day.[31] Martha was of French descent (with a last name difficult to pronounce and more difficult to spell: Delesdernier), while Richard came from

---

[30] The site can usually be visited during tourist season.

[31] Brian Cuthbertson, *The Old Attorney General: A Biography of Richard John Uniacke* (Halifax, NS: Nimbus Publishing Ltd., 1980), 62–63.

an aristocratic Irish family that traced their lineage to the County of Cork in the thirteenth century. At the time of their marriage on May 3, 1775, Martha had virtually no education and was not yet thirteen, while her twenty-one-year-old husband was a well-educated lawyer.[32] Richard's law practice led the couple to settle in the port city of Halifax, which had been founded in 1749. In 1797, Uniacke became the Attorney General, an office he would hold until his death in 1830. The early 1790s saw the purchase of a large property on Argyle Street, where this couple and their growing family soon moved into a new home. It stood where the *Chronicle Herald* building was formerly located. Close by was St. Paul's Anglican Church, where the family worshipped and where Richard, Martha, and their oldest daughter Mary are buried in the church crypt.[33]

Richard Uniacke's plan to build a large house on Argyle was a good one. He and his wife became the parents of twelve children, with one dying at or near birth. Being a fourth-generation Protestant, Richard raised his family with strong moral and religious values. The stubborn Irishman was far from perfect, having a choleric temperament and volatile temper, but even so, it is regrettable that many people know little about the man or the times in which he lived.[34]

Uniacke had little time for the philosophers of his time, who recommended that children be taught only what their reason could comprehend. He rightly concluded that such an education makes men slaves to their passions and perpetrators of every kind of wickedness. He felt that education should be controlled by the church, and he had a strong and unwavering conviction that the principles of religion and morality should be taught to children from an early age.

In 1805, he published what came to be known as *Uniacke's Laws*, which were copied and distributed to all legislators each year. He refused to have his children raised in a moral and religious vacuum, and he encouraged others to follow his example. His conservative philosophy is strongly reflected in this part of his laws:

> It has been our misfortune to live at a period, during which every act has been used to destroy the principles of true religion, and to subvert the rules of civil government. The Christian religion, which is our sure guide to the worship of the true God; the allegiance of subjects to the King; the natural love of our country; the union of husband and wife; the duties of parent and child; the affection of brothers and sisters; and the attachment of friends and countrymen, have been, by impious and

---

[32] Ibid., 5.
[33] Ibid., 133.
[34] Ibid. 12.

wicked men, styled prejudices originating in the human mind from the errors of a false education.[35]

For nearly half a century, his laws were a standard reference for members of the Assembly, the governing body in Halifax.

It seems that while Richard was rough and demanding, his wife had a gentle and persuasive nature that provided balance and stability for their large family. Each evening, Richard prayed with his children and gave them his blessing. Even as they grew into adulthood, they often gathered at their father's bedroom door to receive his blessing when they were at his home for a summer visit.

Trying to nail down a definite conversion experience in Richard's Uniacke's religious journey is a difficult task. Many of his personal papers were destroyed following his death, leaving us dependent on secondary sources which may be somewhat prejudicial. His sixth-generation descendant and biographer, Brian Cuthbertson, insists that the "old Attorney General," as he was called by his peers, did not have an affinity for the strong evangelical fervour becoming more evident in the early part of the nineteenth century.[36] There is little doubt that he had heard about the ministry of Henry Alline, the eighteenth-century charismatic preacher from Falmouth, Nova Scotia, who singlehandedly transformed the religious landscape of the province.

Uniacke was a close friend of Simeon Perkins, the well-known merchant, civic leader, and diarist from Liverpool, Nova Scotia. Perkins wrote approvingly of Henry Alline and often provided lodging for the itinerant preacher from Falmouth. (The reader will be interested to know that the 18th century home of Simeon Perkins, still stands, and can be revisited during tourist season.) The following words came from a man who held Alline in high esteem, and who was obviously deeply moved by what he observed. It is reasonable to assume that the Liverpool businessman would share his enthusiasm with his close friends, including Richard Uniacke.

On Sunday, February 16, 1783, Alline preached his last sermons in Liverpool. Perkins's moving response sensitively reflected the response of his community:

Mr Alline preached both parts of the day & evening... Mr. Alline made a long Speech, Very Sensible, Advising all Sorts of People to a Religious Life, & gave many directions for their outward walk... Never did I behold Such an Appearance of the Spirit of God moving upon the

---

[35] Ibid., 42–43.
[36] Ibid., 98.

people Since the time of the Great Religious Stir in New England many years ago.[37]

We do know that for a time Uniacke gravitated between the dissident churches of that time and the Church of England. After much turmoil, he finally settled at St. Paul's in 1801 and cut all ties with the dissenters. His biographer relates that "he was now fully convinced of Christian doctrine."[38]

Some time after Uniacke fully committed to the ministry at St. Paul's, the church suffered a severe split, leaving the church hopelessly divided. One of the factions was led by Uniacke, and the reluctant fallout left him distraught and disillusioned with churches in general. His attendance became erratic afterward, especially after a large group left St. Paul's en masse and founded the Granville Street Baptist Church.

The Anglican Church of Uniacke's day was a strange mixture of evangelicals, moderates, formalists, and curious religious observers with little or no interest in the gospel. Some in Halifax of the early nineteenth century attended church as an arena of influence for their own political advantage. Whatever Richard Uniacke's motives may have been, it is beyond our limited ability to make an accurate judgment. What is known is that the evangelical movement was a major influence on people's lives, including the family of the Attorney General. His son Richard John was part of a faction that left St. Paul's and attached themselves to St. George's Chapel, an Anglican congregation with strong evangelical convictions, and by 1827 had founded their own parish, rejecting all contrasting influence from St. Paul's. Richard John Uniacke joined his namesake in this departure but soon returned to St. Paul's, perhaps feeling too advanced in years to make such a major transition.

It is my opinion that Uniacke faced the same dilemma with worship style as many professing Christians do now, nearly two centuries later. St. Paul's of that time seems to have been faithful to the teachings of the Bible and presenting the tenets of the gospel to their people. It seems unlikely that Uniacke would have attended any church that did not present the objective truths of the Word of God. He had no interest in what we label today as liberal theology. Within the Anglican Church was a kind of waffling between high church and low church forms of service, paralleled with a strong emphasis on traditional form versus a more informal approach. Does this sound remotely

[37] George A. Rawlyk, ed., *The Sermons of Henry Alline* (Hantsport, NS: Lancelot Press Ltd., 1986), 16.
[38] Cuthbertson, *The Old Attorney General*, 80.

akin to the present? Denominations aside, it is probably fair to say that few issues occupy us more in our day than the style of worship we adopt as a local church.

It is interesting to note that even though Uniacke's chosen place of worship was being ripped apart, this time of upheaval saw his son Robert Fitzgerald become soundly converted and enter the gospel ministry. How this affected his father is unknown.

All indications are that Richard Uniacke preferred a very formal type of worship that some of us would find stifling. His financial status, political loyalties, lofty position as Attorney General, aristocratic family ancestry, and his own personality of stern resolve and high degree of strict organization all positioned him to adopt a worship style that was highly formal and predictable but deeply personal and meaningful. Uniacke could see change around him in all the churches, but his affinity with the more traditional form of worship, as well as his deeply rooted social status, kept him tied to his own church.

During the last century, Harold Lindsell wrote two books that rocked the evangelical world, *The Bible in the Balance* and *The Battle for the Bible*. Asserting that the evangelical scene was in disarray and division, he made his case by stating that many of our leaders had abandoned the authority of the Bible, making way for every kind of questionable doctrine under the banner of evangelicalism. He called for a return to biblical authority in the churches, suggesting that evangelicals had been betrayed by many of the more prominent leaders, whom he did not hesitate to name.

The early evangelicals were fully convinced of the truth of the Bible, and it was preached with authority. They were also committed to a culture of soul-winning, of which we hear little today. There was also a time when the general populace had respect for the Bible, even if not always embracing its teaching on a personal level. We now live in a society that is hostile to the Bible and has little regard or respect for its precepts.

I may draw some fire here, but I have never been convinced that Canada or the United States have ever been Christian nations. Patriotism is commendable, but this does not make any nation Christian; neither does the adoption of democratic principles or the acceptance of religious freedom. To equate any of these dynamics with being Christian is being naïve about human nature and turning a blind eye to the realities of historical record. Even so, there was a time in our country when the biblical view of life was freely expressed with no major repercussions from the general population.

I will submit that Uniacke's laws would not be acceptable to our legislators of today. We have now redefined the concepts of family and marriage. God is now what you make Him to be, which will not necessarily be the God of the Bible. I will go further and suggest that much of the preaching of the past would not only be unacceptable to our postmodern culture, but sadly would not find a home in our churches either. The reference point in those bygone days was the Bible; however, today's Christian is being asked to attend and support no end of movements, seminars, management courses, self-help groups, and church growth conferences without anybody asking the really tough questions relative to the credibility of the speaker and/or concern for biblical content. The overload of emphasis on love, sensitivity, tolerance, and respect has tied the hands of Bible believers.

CHAPTER FOUR

The Battle Rages

Many of our evangelical leaders and Bible commentators stumble from the very beginning, in the book of Genesis. Every kind of literary idiom is adopted to either accommodate evolution and long ages within the creation account or dismiss a literal creation altogether. When we move on to the account of the flood, the same hijinks are employed to dismiss the universality of the catastrophe while confining the water to a limited geographical area.

It would be surprising to many Christians how many of our evangelical preachers no longer believe in the concept of an eternal hell. The only way to dismiss this doctrine is to deny the plain teaching of the Bible. If hell is questioned, can we even be sure of heaven as taught in the Scriptures?

> C. S. Lewis said, "I have met no people who fully disbelieved in Hell and also had a living and life-giving belief in Heaven." The biblical teaching on both destinations stands or falls together.[39]

These words from Mark Galli get straight to the point:

---

[39] Randy Alcorn, *Heaven* (Wheaton, IL: Tyndale House, 2004), 26.

Though Christ's words about hell are clear, emphatic, and repeated, our temptation is to think he didn't mean what he said. But isn't the most obvious conclusion that he really did? And that the doctrine of hell isn't a ballot measure, and God doesn't give us a vote? Hell is dreadful, but it is not evil—it's a place where evil gets punished. Something can be profoundly disturbing yet still be moral. Hell is moral because a good God must punish evil. C.S. Lewis said of hell, "There is no doctrine which I would more willingly remove from Christianity than this, if it lay in my power. But it has the full support of Scripture and, specially, of our Lord's own words; it has always been held by Christendom; and it has the support of reason." Dorothy Sayers, another broad-minded Christian, claimed, "We cannot repudiate Hell without altogether repudiating Christ."[40]

The moral arena must not be overlooked here. Whole denominations are now faced with the red hot issues of homosexuality and gay marriage. Any discussion about these subjects, even among Christians, can turn into an emotional firestorm. The gay pride parades now becoming annual events in many of our towns and cities are designed to break our resistance and silence our voices. Flaunting their chosen lifestyle publicly, they dare anyone to show their disapproval.

Sodom and Gomorrah were destroyed because of homosexuality, but even within our evangelical churches there are pockets of influence determined to revise the Bible, telling us that the real issue in those cities was hospitality, not sexual orientation. There is ample proof that homosexuality is neither a sickness nor uncontrollable, as many are leaving this lifestyle permanently and a goodly number are being converted to Christ.

While many of our churches are filled with strife and division, in which people argue unendingly about worship style and Bible translations, we have not given God's Word an opportunity to speak to our hearts. Problems in our churches reflect the difficulties of our society. We are living in a dying culture that has lost all sense of purpose, meaning, and fulfillment. Whereas past generations believed that truth could be found, we are presently left in the land of despair, convinced that truth cannot be found. A culture without the Bible is a culture without principles, without conscience, and without hope.

Our society is falling apart at the seams and the answer is the objective truth found in the Word of God. Only there do we see a loving God who longs to

[40] Mark Galli, *God Wins: Heaven, Hell and Why the Good News Is Better than Love Wins* (Carol Stream, IL: Tyndale House, Inc., 2011), ix.

have a relationship with fallen people. Only there do we read of God's plan of redemption for the human race. Only there do we find that life has purpose as we place faith and trust in the Lord Jesus Christ.

The church has been stupefied by the humanistic thinking that has found its way into our programs, pews, and pulpits. No longer convinced that we have a message from God, every kind of intellectual manipulation is used to soften or eliminate biblical teaching offensive to our culture or the worldly wise Christian who is far more in love with the spirit of this age than with the Spirit of God who has given us the inspired Scriptures.

We are in the Truth War, and the battle is raging. Some think we are called to open up diplomatic relations with human philosophies and anti-Christian ideas rather than wage war on all that is contrary to the Word of God. Hear the words of Martin Luther, who was forced into hiding after listing no less than ninety-five errors of the Roman Catholic Church:

> If I profess with the loudest voice and clearest exposition every portion of the truth of God except precisely that little point which the world and the devil are at that moment attacking, I am not confessing Christ, however boldly I may be professing Christ. Where the battle rages, there the loyalty of the soldier is proved; and to be steady on the battlefield besides, is mere flight and disgrace if he flinches at THAT point.[41]

Before going the next step of this journey, I leave you with these words from Charles Spurgeon, which are quite revealing indeed when we consider that they were written by a Baptist about the Baptists of his day in England, in the latter part of the nineteenth century:

> No lover of the Gospel can conceal from himself the fact that the days are evil… What doctrine remains to be abandoned? What other truth to be the object of contempt? A new religion has been initiated which is no more Christianity than chalk is cheese, and this religion, being destitute of moral honesty, palms itself off as the old faith with slight improvements, and on this plea usurps pulpits which were erected for gospel preaching. The Atonement is scouted [rejected], the inspiration of Scripture is derided, the Holy Ghost is degraded into an influence, the punishment of sin is turned into fiction, and the Resurrection into a

---

[41] Harold Lindsell, *The Battle for the Bible* (Grand Rapids: Zondervan, 1979), 201.

myth, and yet these enemies of our faith expect us to call them brethren, and maintain a confederacy with them.[42]

The indestructibility of God's Word is aptly described in the following poem:

GOD'S WORD
I paused last eve beside the blacksmith's door,
And heard the anvil ring, the vesper's chime,
And looking in I saw upon the floor
Old hammers, worn with beating years of time.
"How many anvils have you had?" said I,
"To wear and batter all these hammers so?"
"Just one," he answered. Then with twinkling eye:
"The anvil wears the hammers out, you know."
And so, I thought, the anvil of God's Word
For ages skeptics' blows have beat upon,
But though the noise of falling blows was heard
The anvil is unchanged; the hammers gone.[43]
– John Clifford

HARD PLACES OF SCRIPTURE
"The Bible is full of errors and contradictions!" This is a favourite attack levelled against the Bible by skeptics, but is this statement justified? We, as Bible believers, are very much aware of certain difficulties in the Bible, or what the Geneva Bible translators called the "hard places," but these are a far cry from being errors, mistakes, or contradictions.[44] After all, the Bible is a divine book and we are all too human.

Bible readers are often puzzled not only by the difficulty of the language, but by the profoundness of the message. Bishop Westcott famously stated, "God was pleased to leave difficulties upon the surface of Scripture, that men might be forced to look below the surface."[45]

In response to the charges against the reliability of God's Word, W.A. Criswell gives us this enlightening observation:

---

[42] Ibid., 67.

[43] John Clifford in *The Treasury of Religious Verse*, comp. Donald T. Kauffman (Westwood, NJ: Fleming H. Revell, 1962), 49.

[44] Lloyd E. Berry, introduction to *The Geneva Bible: A Facsimile of the 1560 Edition* (Peabody, MA: Hendrickson, 2007), 12.

[45] Andreas J. Kostenberger and David A. Croteau, eds., *Which Bible Translation Should I Use?* (Paris, ON: B&H Publishing Group, 2012), 120.

As we confront the difficulties of the Bible, we are ever to remember that we are not to apply standards to the Scriptures which do not suit them. The Scriptures were not written to give us a course in mathematics or in biology; nor were the Scriptures written to recount a full history of the chosen people of God or to narrate a full biography of Jesus. God speaks to us through the Scriptures not in order to make us mathematicians or biologists or historians, but in order to make us children of our Heavenly Father.[46]

It is my experience that some of the most vocal critics of the Scriptures have spent very little time reading them or making a concentrated effort to become familiar with their contents. The most vicious attacks are usually levelled against the Old Testament, but some of those same individuals often haul in their horns when reminded that the Old Testament is fully supported by the New Testament. You will also find that some critics are experts at mimicking other critics. Don't be afraid to ask where they got their negative remarks and encourage them to carefully read the Scripture in question. In too many cases, they have never read the passage they feel free to scrutinize. This can be an excellent opportunity to share the gospel and show the love of Christ.

WHERE DID CAIN GET HIS BRIDE?

Some of the most common difficulties with the Bible are also the most longstanding. Since the early church era, there have been questions about the book of Genesis, especially Cain's journey to the land of Nod, where he finds a wife (Genesis 4:15–17). One writer has verbalized in excellent fashion where the real problem lies. He says, "Our trouble, therefore, lies not in the Bible but in what man has done to the Bible."[47] The question that has been so often asked is the wrong question based on a total misunderstanding of the first five chapters of Genesis.

Where did Cain get his wife? The answer is in plain sight. When the Scripture is properly read, the real question is this: from the twenty thousand women on the earth at the time, how did Cain settle on a suitable life partner when they were all related?

We must realize that the Bible gives us only some of the details of any given situation. We are given what we need to know, not necessarily all that we want

---

[46] W.A. Criswell, *Why I Preach That the Bible is Literally True* (Nashville: Broadman Press, 1969), 61–62.

[47] Ibid., 63.

to know. Reading the early chapters of Genesis as a chronological account is a common error. The second chapter is not another version of the creation but gives added details to the original account in the first chapter. An unbiased reader will read the fourth and fifth chapters of Genesis as parallel passages, not as a verse-by-verse chronological account.

Many Bible scholars believe that by the time Cain went looking for a wife, there were at least thirty-five thousand descendants of Adam and Eve on the planet, and a strong and stable civilized society was quickly taking shape due to their exile from the Garden of Eden. To this day, even secular historians, for the most part, cite the large landmass which we now call Iraq as the cradle of the human race. The land on both sides of the Euphrates River has always received special attention by serious students of history, which lends strong credence to the Genesis account.

Or perhaps we should say that the Bible supports the historians.[48]

Before entertaining other considerations that point to a trustworthy Bible, Criswell gives us these words to ponder:

> There is no contradiction in the Bible to any fact of science. The physical universe, the mystery of planetary and stellar movements, the constitution of man, the world of plant and animal life, the mystery of life itself, and the constitution of the earth in material forms and forces— all of these things that we know in science are in perfect harmony with what is presented in the Bible. There is topographical, geographical, chronological, and historical trustworthiness in the Word of God that is according to His infallible knowledge.[49]

Christians have nothing to fear from those who attack God's Word.

We have already seen a number of instances where the enemies of God's Word have had to retreat from their position in the face of overwhelming evidence that supports the truth of Scripture. The child of God can read the Word of God with full confidence that the Bible is rich with truth and free from error.

THE MIRACLE OF ONENESS
The unity of the Scriptures is further proof that the Bible is worthy of our complete trust. Here we have, in one volume, sixty-six books written by over forty human

---

[48] Ibid., 62–64.
[49] Ibid., 65.

authors in a period stretching over sixteen centuries. Though coming from a wide variety of cultures and backgrounds, all of the writers present the same unified theme—namely, God's relationship to the human race. God's plan to redeem men and women from the jaws of Satan and eternal death in the lake of fire, thereby restoring their standing with God following the fall of our first parents, runs from the early chapters of Genesis to the end of Revelation.

Here is Criswell's assessment:

> It would be impossible for the man who wrote the first pages to have had the slightest knowledge of what the man would write 1,500 years after he was born. Yet his miscellaneous collection of heterogeneous writings is not only unified in one Book but so unified by God that no one even thinks of it today as anything else than one Book, and indeed, one Book it is, the miracle of all literary unity. There is a perfect harmony throughout the Scriptures from the first verse in Genesis to the last verse in the Revelation. The profound ethical and spiritual values in the Bible agree. The more one really studies the Bible the more one is convinced that behind the many authors there is one overruling, controlling mind.[50]

How are we to explain the endurance of the sacred text we call the Bible? Any honest mind must surely acknowledge that this is no ordinary piece of literature. Its very existence must cause us to ponder its presence among us.

> There never was any order given to any man to plan the Bible. Nor was there any concerted plan on the part of men to write the Bible. The way in which the Bible gradually developed through the centuries is one of the mysteries of time... The Bible was written on two continents, in countries hundreds of miles apart. One man wrote one part of the Bible in Syria; another man wrote another part in Arabia; a third man wrote another portion in Italy and in Greece. They wrote in the desert of Sinai, in the wilderness of Judea, in the cave of Adullam, in the public prison of Rome, on the Isle of Patmos, in the palaces of Mount Zion and Shushan, by the rivers of Babylon and on the banks of the Chebar. Such a variety of places and circumstances were the various bits of this strange mosaic created! No literary phenomenon in the world can be compared with it... Although the Bible is a volume of sixty-six books written by

---

[50] Ibid, 96.

forty different men, treating such a large variety of themes as to cover nearly the whole range of human inquiry, yet we find the Book is one book. It is the Book, not the books. It is *the* Bible.[51]

The unity of the message of the Bible is what draws us and demands our utmost intention.

The miracle of the unity of the Bible is the unity of one organic whole. The Decalogue demands the Sermon on the Mount; Isaiah's prophecies make necessary the narrative of the gospel writers. Daniel fits into the Revelation as bone fits into socket. Leviticus explains and is explained by the epistle to the Hebrews. The Psalms express the highest anticipations and longings of comfort we find in Christ Jesus. When we read the last chapters of the Revelation, we find ourselves mysteriously touching the first chapters of Genesis. As you survey the whole circle of the Bible, you find you have been following the perimeter of a golden ring. The extremities actually bend around, touch, and blend.[52]

The writers of the Bible comprise a fascinating group of authors. They include fishermen, farmers, herdsmen, tax collectors, and physicians. Because they wrote over a combined period of fifteen hundred years, they were very obviously unable to collaborate on what they wrote. Without any hint of pride or showmanship, these forty writers wrote accounts which they never doubted were all true. With the few exceptions of Moses, Solomon, Paul, Luke, and James, they were not what one would call well-educated or sophisticated. They were a motley bunch who felt strangely led by an Unseen Presence.

They made no disclaimers, no apologies. They never said anything like "Now, this may sound ridiculous, but this really is the Word of God." Instead, they repeatedly and unabashedly claimed to be writing God's Word. One Bible scholar estimates that in the Old Testament alone there are over 2,600 such claims. If you want to break it down, there are 682 claims in the Pentateuch [the first five books of the OT], 1,307 claims in the Prophetic books, 418 claims in the historical books and 195 claims in the poetic books.[53]

---

[51] Ibid., 93–96. [49] Ibid., 97–98.
[52] Ibid., 97–98.
[53] John MacArthur, *Why Believe the Bible?* (Ventura, CA: Gospel Light/Regal, 2007), 65.

There are individuals in our society who continually ridicule the sacred Scriptures without ever considering the evidence. Most people have a positive take on parts of the Bible but have reservations about the more difficult passages, those portions they find offensive or objectionable for one reason or another. In other words, the Bible does not always agree with our moral or social values. Some suggest that some of the Bible makes good sense and may have a divine source, but some of it is just the opinions and thoughts of well-meaning men and women. As one writer ably points out, this puts all of us on the horns of a huge dilemma:

[The] "partly God's Word, partly man's word" position leads to a view of the Bible that says that part of it is of great value but there are also other parts that are full of errors and that are "utterly useless and valueless"… we are then faced with a very basic question: "Who decides what is true? Who decides what is of value? How can you discriminate and differentiate between the great facts that are true and those that are false? How can you differentiate between and separate facts from teaching? How can you separate this essential message of the Bible from the background in which it is presented?… The whole Bible comes to us and offers itself to us in exactly the same way. There is no hint, no suspicion of a suggestion that parts of it are important and parts are not. They all come to us in the same form… "We decide that one portion conforms to the message, which we believe, and that another does not. We are left still with the position, in spite of all the talk about a new situation today, that man's knowledge and man's understanding are the final arbiter and the final court of appeal.[54]

---

[54] Ibid., 18.

CHAPTER FIVE

Dust on the Bible

Then Ezra the priest brought the law before the assembly of men, women and all who could listen with understanding, on the first day of the seventh month. He read from it before the square which was in front of the Water Gate from early morning until midday, in the presence of men and women, those who could understand; and all the people were attentive to the book of the law. (Nehemiah 8:2–3, NASB)

The last half of the seventh century B.C. saw the southern kingdom of Judah caught up in the throes of major political upheaval and widespread religious apostasy. The northern kingdom had been destroyed by the Assyrians the century before. Many Jews had been deported, while others were forced to intermingle with the vast numbers of foreigners who swelled the population of Samaria.

While the Assyrians were losing their hold on the area, another invader had to be reckoned with—the powerful Babylonians. Fearing for their political future, the Egyptians had aligned themselves with the Assyrians while Judah desperately struggled to cut a deal with the new enemy and save her kingdom. Into this boiling political cauldron came eight-year-old Josiah as the new king of Judah. Descended from King David's royal line, he was destined to be the greatest king in Judah since the time that his famous ancestor had ruled the united kingdom of Israel.

The reign of Josiah followed the two-year inept rule of his father Amon, who was assassinated in his own house by his domestic servants. Josiah's grandfather Manasseh had ruled for fifty-five years, and though experiencing a spiritual awakening in later life, he had by then led the nation into such moral and religious debauchery that his best efforts could not reverse the inevitable judgment upon the nation. King Josiah would soon find out just how far his people had drifted from God. He would learn that under his grandfather's rule, the nation had turned to numerous vile idolatrous practices and the Word of God had been all but destroyed.

THE SCRIPTURES RECOVERED

All of this is played out in 2 Kings 22–23. Josiah's family credentials left something to be desired, but his spiritual qualifications were commendable.

> *He did right in the sight of the Lord and walked in all the way of his father David, nor did he turn aside to the right or to the left.* (2 Kings 22:2, NASB)

Further testimony is added in 2 Kings 23:2:

> *Before him there was no king like him who turned to the Lord with all his heart and with all his soul and with all his might, according to all the law of Moses; nor did any like him arise after him.* (NASB)

Coming to the throne at the age of eight, we can assume, as do many Bible scholars, that Josiah was accompanied by regents and guardians for the early part of his reign. Apparently raised in an atmosphere of piety and deep love for God, Josiah was made acutely aware of the precarious moral condition of the nation. Instilled with godly values at a young age, his conversion came early. According to 2 Chronicles 34:3, he came to faith at sixteen years of age, and four years later he began a series of major reforms in an effort to save his nation from the wrath of a holy God.[55]

At twenty-six years of age, Josiah expresses personal interest in the temple by sending Shapham the scribe to inquire about temple offerings. While there, Hilkiah, the high priest, made an astounding statement: *"I have found the book of the law in the house of the Lord"* (2 Kings 22:8). The Word of God was hidden

---

[55] *Liberty Bible Commentary* (Lynchburg, VA: The Old Time Gospel Hour, 1983), 739–740.

under the rubble, possibly placed there by a priest to protect it from harm during the years of spiritual declension under Josiah's grandfather Manasseh.

The law found by Hilkiah was possibly a copy of Deuteronomy, but some believe it included all five books of Moses. Jimmy Swaggart shares the following:

> Actually, this was the original Pentateuch which had been written by Moses, and had been laid up by the side of the Ark. It probably was hidden there during the reigns of Manasseh and Amon, because of their wickedness in turning against Jehovah. It had been written by Moses from the Mouth of God more than 800 years before Josiah was born. So, this was an incredible discovery.[56]

Whatever edition it was, Josiah read it before the people (2 Kings 23:1–3). Having begun spiritual renewal six years earlier, he now applied the letter of the law in an unprecedented manner, armed with the authority of God's Word. One writer comments,

> Every major or minor revival of true faith has involved a rediscovery of the teaching of the Word of God. The great Reformation of the sixteenth century was no exception.[57]

He repaired the temple, destroyed the altar of Baal, removed heathen idols, tore down the houses of male prostitutes, and removed the mediums, wizards, and soothsayers. He also presided over one of the greatest Passover services ever held and led his people in a massive service of repentance. By the time of his death on the battlefield in 610 B.C., Josiah had led his nation in a huge step toward spiritual recovery, but the sins of his grandfather were such that God had determined to *"remove Judah… cast off Jerusalem, this city which I have chosen, and the temple of which I said, "My name shall be there"* (2 Kings 23:27, NASB).[58]

Less than twenty-five years following the end of Josiah's reign, key historical events (which are well documented in both secular and biblical sources) began to unfold. In 605 B.C., the Egyptians, who were already making incursions into Judah in the time of Josiah, were decisively defeated by the Babylonians. The

---

[56] Jimmy Swaggart, *The Expositor's Study Bible* (Baton Rouge, LA: Jimmy Swaggart Ministries, 2006), 671. Giant Print Edition

[57] William MacDonald, *Believer's Bible Commentary* (Nashville, TN: Thomas Nelson Publishers, 1992), 464.

[58] Ibid., 417–418.

deportation of Jews into the far reaches of Nebuchadnezzar's empire commenced in 606 B.C., during the reign of Jehoiakim, the self-centred king who brazenly burned a portion of God's Word (Jeremiah 36:22–32). Among the initial group of captives was a young man called Daniel. A second deportation in 597 B.C. included Ezekiel, who would receive his call to ministry long after he was taken out of Judah. The final blow came in 586 B.C., when the temple was totally destroyed and many more Jews were forced to leave their homeland.[59]

As these dark days of war and destruction spread over the land, God continued to speak to His people through the ministry of Jeremiah, whose prophetic voice was heard in the streets of Jerusalem for over forty years. Known as the "weeping prophet," Jeremiah began warning God's people of God's impending judgment a year after Josiah began his spiritual reforms. Beginning with Josiah, Jeremiah preached and wept his way through the reigns of the last five kings of Judah. He was never deported but probably ended his final days in Egypt.[60] I cannot help but think that Josiah's determination and desire to turn his nation back to God and His Word exercised profound and positive influence in the lives of three of the greatest Old Testament prophets, all of whom were living during Josiah's reign and whose ministries produced a large part of the Old Testament Scriptures.

Named after the author, Jeremiah is the longest prophetic book in the Bible and is followed up by Lamentations, which is also ascribed to the "weeping prophet."

Probably the most colourful among the prophets, Ezekiel and his wife lived in their own home in Tel-Abib, probably southeast of Babylon. According to the book that bears his name, Ezekiel was a priest who received his special calling among the exiles by the river Chebar in 593 B.C. (Ezekiel 1:1–3).[61]

Some of the most familiar stories known to Christians are found in the book of Daniel. According to sources outside the Bible, Daniel was of noble or royal descent. His is one of the most significant prophetic books of the Old Testament, providing an indispensable backdrop to New Testament prophecy. His long and active life lasted well into the reign of Cyrus, which means he witnessed the fall of Babylon in 539 B.C. Daniel's name means "God is my judge."[62]

---

[59] Merrill C. Tenney, "Captivity," *Zondervan's Pictorial Bible Dictionary* (Grand Rapids: Zondervan, 1967), 147.

[60] J.D. Douglas, ed., "The Five Kings," *The New Bible Dictionary* (Downers Grove, IL: IVP Academic, 1997), 550–552.

[61] John MacArthur, ed., *The MacArthur Study Bible* (Nashville, TN: Word Publishing/Thomas Nelson, 1997), 1150.

[62] Merrill F. Unger, *Unger's Bible Dictionary* (Chicago: Moody Press, 1966), 237–238.

These three prophets, along with the young king who reintroduced God's Word to the people, were used of God to keep the people of Israel reminded of their responsibility to take God's truth to the nations around them. These men were all students of God's law and each was uniquely positioned in history to be used of God in their generation. The policies of Josiah gave Judah some degree of respite but could not bring full recovery from generations of spiritual ineptitude prior to his ascension to the throne. None of the last four kings of the southern kingdom had strength of character or spiritual vitality.

This terse statement sums it up: "At his [Josiah's] death Judah would see no more good kings. It was all spiritual degeneration from this point on."[63] The last of the four was Zedekiah, who was nothing more than a puppet for Nebuchadnezzar. His rebellion against the Babylonians, who already had Jerusalem in their grip, prompted the besiegers to break into the city and eliminate the last vestige of resistance. Zedekiah attempted to escape, but was captured and brought back to Nebuchadnezzar for punishment. He was forced to witness the execution of his sons and then his eyes were gouged out. He was finally taken in chains to Babylon where he died (Jeremiah 52:4–11; 39:1–7).[64]

The final devastation of Jerusalem struck at the very heart of Jewish consciousness, but even in the aftermath of those dark days the voice of Jeremiah could still be heard. Many would recall the noble efforts of Josiah to save the nation from such a fate, and when they were transported to the far-flung frontiers of Nebuchadnezzar's kingdom, Ezekiel was there to remind them of the majesty of their God. When some were assimilated into the royal customs of the capital city of Babylon, they would learn from Daniel how to conduct themselves as God's chosen people in the midst of pagan culture and heathen protocol.

With the temple demolished, the priesthood lost their centre, which meant the suspension of the sacrificial offerings. With the loss of the monarchy, the people had no leader. Richard Elliot Friedman gives us a sense of the emotional pain and distress that was felt by the Jewish survivors of the Babylonian war machine:

In short, the Babylonian destruction of Judah had brought horrors and tremendous challenges and crisis to this nation. They were forced to reformulate their picture of themselves and of their relationship with their God. They had to find a way to worship Yahweh without a Temple.

[63] H.L. Wilmington, *Wilmington's Guide to the Bible* (Wheaton, IL: Tyndale House, 1981), 162.
[64] Ibid., 163.

They had to find leadership without a king. They had to learn to live as a minority ethnic group in great empires. They had to determine what their relationship was to their homeland. And they had to live with their defeat.[65]

Like Josiah, we need to lift the Bible out of the dust of neglect and read it as we never have before. While it is true that numerous books are being written about the Bible, there is a real danger of ignoring the Bible itself. Never before in history have so many study helps, study books, and study Bibles been available to the church, but our reading habits are far inferior to those of our ancestors, and our overall knowledge of God's Word is far below that of past generations.

This is Robert Chapman's description of the Bible:

This book contains the mind of God, the state of man, the way of salvation, the doom of sinners, and the happiness of believers.......
Read it to be wise, believe it to be safe, and practice it to be holy. It is the traveler's map, the pilgrim's staff, the pilot's compass, the soldier's sword... Read it slowly, frequently, prayerfully... It involves the highest responsibility, rewards the greatest labour, and condemns all who will trifle with its sacred contents.[66]

What is too frequently apparent is that too many believers fail to give the Bible the quality attention it so rightly deserves. This is evidenced by the continued neglect of its sacred contents. Ponder the words of John MacArthur:

They [believers] know the Bible is important and that it should have priority and authority in their lives, but they don't make much personal use of it. They neglect its teachings altogether or they slip by, seldom opening the Bible for themselves, and depend on pastors, teachers or speakers to "explain it to them." They make little application of what the Scriptures teach. The Bible remains a mysterious, somewhat confusing rulebook that they are supposed to swallow bravely, like a bitter vitamin every morning before breakfast.[67]

---

[65] Richard Elliot Friedman, *Who Wrote the Bible?* (New York, NY: Summit Books, 1987), 155.
[66] Kroll, *Back to the Bible*, 16.
[67] MacArthur, *Why Believe the Bible?*, 11.

Woodrow Kroll of *Back to the Bible* asked the question that cries out for an answer: "Why is the only book God ever wrote so little read by God's people?"[68] It is now our task to address this most urgent concern.

- Our educational system has been dumbed down. Our electronically developed countries rely increasingly on oral and non-print visual technology such as video, radio, television, and computer to access information. Kroll suggests that there is a "downward spiral of reading and writing skills… and a generally lessened ability to think, read, and do research."[69] As our worship services have moved from hymnals to transparencies to PowerPoint, we have sent the wrong message—namely, that it is no longer necessary to carry our Bibles to church. The difficulty only increases as we return to our homes to be feted by many hours of religious broadcasting on the radio and television while our Bibles are rarely read.[70]
- We have not made Bible reading a priority in our busy contemporary lives. The reading of our Bibles must become a daily activity on our calendar of events.[71]
- Pastors and Christian educators are attending schools where theology is largely replaced with psychology, management skills, and church growth strategies.[72]
- More than one Christian has noted that expositional preaching, where the text is exposed and explained in detail, is sadly lacking in many pulpits.[73]
- Pastors need to take at least some responsibility for the lack of Bible knowledge in our churches. Woodrow Kroll pulls no punches here, saying, "Many pastors today look more like stand-up comics than expositors of the Word of Life."[74]
- Our postmodern culture is not friendly to the Word of God. This can prove to be intimidating to a Bible-believing and Bible-reading Christian who walks out of a meaningful worship service on Sunday morning and twenty-four hours later finds himself in a cultural atmosphere that is hostile to God and His Word. Our postmodern culture has persuaded the masses that everything is relative and truth is nowhere to be found. In this context,

[68] Kroll, *Back to the Bible*, 15.
[69] Ibid., 78.
[70] Ibid., 78–79.
[71] Ibid., 163–172.
[72] Ibid., 62.
[73] Ibid., 134–135.
[74] Ibid., 135.

Wood Kroll states what is painfully obvious: "God's eternal truth has no place in such a world."[75] This answers why biblical literacy is in sharp decline in North America.

There are sharp, obvious disparities between postmodern beliefs and the Bible. The problem is that we live in a postmodern world, and we don't live in our Bible. That means even Christians will slowly but surely become increasingly like the world and less like the Savior. That's why getting back to the Bible is so important for us, for the church, and for our society. Our future depends on it.[76]

The following is an interesting excerpt from the opening chapter of *The Unknown Bible*, published in 1926 and authored by Conrad Henry Moehlman.

I am a copy of a library of books called the Bible. It is proclaimed from pulpit and printed page that I am the best seller in the western world. Some five million entire Bibles and parts of Bibles are published each year. I have been translated into hundreds of languages and dialects. I appear in raised type that the blind may read me. I have influenced the development of medicine, law, art, literature, and the vocabulary of the peoples. My cultural significance cannot be overestimated. And yet, I am the unknown Bible. I was purchased in a bookshop on Main Street. I am owned by one whose name was carefully inscribed upon my first page. Occasionally I am consulted when the family is interested in running down the minister's text. Most of my life had been passed up here on this shelf. Sometimes they take me down to press pansies between my pages. When the family circle is invaded by death, they turn for consolation to the ninetieth psalm or the fourteenth chapter of a gospel that bears the name of John. My proprietors are constantly apologizing for me. They write articles in the daily paper and monthly magazine about me. But they woefully neglect me. I am one of the least appreciated books in their library. I wonder why![77]

Time has not in any way diminished the relevance of these words for our

---

[75] Ibid., 84.
[76] Ibid., 90.
[77] Conrad Henry Moehlman, *The Unknown Bible: The Sources and Selection of the Scripture Canon* (New York, NY: George H. Doran Company, 1926), 13–14. Introduction by Cornelius Woelfkin.

present day. Former president Woodrow Wilson (1856–1924) has given us these thoughtful words to ponder:

I am sorry for the men who do not read the Bible every day; I wonder why they deprive themselves of the strength and of the pleasure.[78]

Another former president, John Quincy Adams, also shares his love for God's Word:

So great is my veneration for the Bible that the earlier my children begin to read it, the more confident will be my hope that they will prove useful citizens to their country, and respectable members of society.[79]

William Huntington (1745–1813) shows his unbounded confidence in the Bible, which stands alone as the bulwark of truth for both time and eternity:

I have sometimes thought, that a nation must be truly blessed, if it were governed by no other laws than those of that blessed book [the Bible]. It is so complete a system, that nothing can be added to it or taken from it. It contains every thing needful to be known and done…

In short, it is a book of law, to shew right and wrong; a book of wisdom, that condemns all folly, and makes the foolish wise: a book of truth, that detects all lies, and confutes all errors; and a book of life, that gives life, and shews the way from everlasting death…

It is the ignorant man's dictionary, and the wise man's directory. It affords knowledge of witty inventions for the humorous, and dark sayings for the grave; and is its own interpreter. It encourages the wise, the warrior, the swift, and the overcomer; and promises an eternal reward to the excellent, the conqueror, the winner, and the prevalent…

And the best of all is, that it promises freedom indeed to all who embrace the truths of it; freedom from the reign of sin, of Satan, and of death: and, except a man receive the truth, the real truth, and that in the love of it, he never shall be able to govern himself, or to bridle his temper, his passions, his tongue, or his sin![80]

[78] Kroll, *Back to the Bible*, 13.
[79] Ibid., 24.
[80] William Huntington, "The History of Little Faith," *Select Works of William Huntington, Volume 1* (Harpenden, UK: Gospel Standard Trust Publications, 1989), 536–539.

CHAPTER SIX

The Church and the Bible

The worldwide influence of the church today can only be attributed to the power that is to be found in the Bible. Every attack upon God's sacred Word has been thwarted throughout the centuries. The sacred page has been banished and burned many times over, but it always rises from the ashes, and its life-giving message continues to transform lives and set the sinner free.

The special qualities of this very special book cannot be ignored, but just what is the Bible? Is it just another book among the many millions made available to humanity? Are its teachings from God, or are they just the figments of wild imaginations? Can the Bible be trusted in its references to history and science? Is it chronologically accurate, or is it open for scrutiny? Are there errors in the Bible, and if so, how blatant are they? Is the creation account a viable option for a culture steeped in evolutionary theory presented as fact? How do we know the Bible is not just another book, like a Charles Dickens novel or a Shakespearean play? If this marvellous volume of sixty-six books is what it claims to be, then we can read it and trust it to be God's pathway to excellence.

Surely, the Bible, which is seen by so many to be fully out of step with our postmodern culture, could not possibly outlast all the arguments raised against it. Nonetheless, not only does this book survive, it continues to thrive in a societal mainstream that has made every effort to disprove its teachings and banish it into oblivion. Bernard Ramm observes,

A thousand times over, the death knell of the Bible has been sounded, the funeral procession formed, the inscription cut on the tombstone, and the committal read. But somehow the corpse never stays put. No other book has been so chopped, sliced, sifted, scrutinized and vilified. What book on philosophy or religion or psychology or belles lettres of classical or modern times has been subject to such a mass attack as the Bible? With such venom and skepticism? With such thoroughness and erudition [knowledge learned by study]? Upon every chapter, line and tenet? The Bible is still loved by millions and studied by millions.[81]

Francois Marie Arouet, commonly known as Voltaire, was an eighteenth-century writer and historian. Born in Paris and educated by the Jesuits, he became increasingly skeptical of the teachings of the Bible.

[Arouet] once said, "Another century and there will be not a Bible on the earth." The century is gone, and the circulation of the Bible is one of the marvels of the age. After he died, his old printing press and the very house where he lived [Ferney, near Geneva] was purchased by the Geneva Bible Society and made a depot for Bibles.[82]

William Foxwell Albright was born of American missionary parents in 1891. This long-time professor at John Hopkins University was, for a time, director of the American School of Oriental Research in Jerusalem. His many excavations of important sites in Palestine made him "one of the greatest and most respected oriental scholars who ever lived."[83] He writes the following:

The reader may rest assured: nothing has been found to disturb a reasonable faith, and nothing has been discovered which can disprove a single theological doctrine... We no longer trouble ourselves with attempts to "harmonize" religion and science, or to "prove" the Bible. The Bible can stand for itself.[84]

MOSES: MAN OF DESTINY

Christians must never forget their indebtedness to the Jewish people. With the possible exception of Luke, all of the biblical authors were Jews. Moses is used

[81] Kroll, *Back to the Bible*, 88.
[82] Wilmington, *Guide to the Bible*, 813.
[83] Ibid.
[84] Ibid.

of God to give us the first five books of the Bible, which are foundational to the Scriptures that follow, both the Old Testament and the New.

In his infancy, Moses was marked for death by the Egyptians, who had ordered every male to be killed at birth. His mother, Jochebed, hid him for three months and, fearing detection, she built a small ark in which she placed little Moses and set him adrift in the marshes. His older sister, Miriam, was left on the shoreline to keep watch over the precious cargo. Shortly afterward, Pharaoh's daughter came down to the river and spotted the ark. She ordered her maid to bring the ark ashore, where she looked upon the baby Moses and decided to take him home.

Miriam, just a little girl, knew how to keep a secret and said nothing about the identity of her baby brother. She asked Pharaoh's daughter if she would like a Jewish woman to care for the baby. After receiving a positive response, Miriam went as commanded and returned with her own mother.

The Egyptian princess knew there would be any number of young Jewish women available to nurse her newly adopted son due to her father's policy of killing all Jewish males at birth. It's what she didn't know that raises the interest level of this story. Jochebed was paid from the coffers of the royal household of Egypt to raise her own son without the Egyptians knowing the connection between her and the baby.

All of this is detailed in the first two chapters of Exodus, but the New Testament fills in missing details, revealing to us the powerful influence of Moses' mother on her little son. Some of the information is an exact match to the passage in Exodus, but a careful reading of Hebrews 11:23–29 tells us that Moses refused to be called the son of Pharaoh's daughter, revealing that his biological mother had taught him well.

This is the same Moses who was used of God to give us the Ten Commandments (Exodus 20). This same Moses was given the pattern for the tabernacle, which became the place of worship for the Israelites during their forty-year wilderness wanderings (Exodus 25–40). But most importantly, this same Moses gave us the first five books of the Old Testament. He was well-qualified for the task. He received his religious training from his godly mother and his highly sophisticated and intellectual training from the superior academic schools of Egypt. His attachment to the royal household gave him the added advantage of a free education. Without the rescue of a little baby from the marshes of the Nile River between three and four thousand years ago, there would be no nation of Israel and no Bible.

The resiliency of the people of Israel is displayed throughout the Bible from Genesis 12 to the present day. Throughout history, they have been constantly hated and harassed by nations that are far larger in both landmass and population, yet they endure.

Scientist and author Alan Hayward points to the major reason why the Germans lost the Second Word War:

> When the Nazi party adopted Hitler's plan to wipe out the Jewish nation, it signed its own death warrant. God had warned the world that He would oppose those who opposed His nation, Israel. By murdering millions of Jews the Nazis were challenging the Almighty to His face. No wonder they lost the war![85]

The ending of hostilities in 1945 left Germany in total ruin. The country was bankrupt and people were dying of starvation. To add to their misery, the victorious allies demanded reparations that the Germans could ill afford.

> Yet the West German Government decided, despite their own people's desperate need for goods and money, to pay hundreds of millions of pounds in compensation to Jews who had suffered through the war. They did not lose by their generosity. The land that lay in ruins in 1945 was, by 1965, almost the richest in Europe.[86]

God has kept the promise he made to Abraham in Genesis 12:3: *"And I will bless them that bless thee, and curse him that curseth thee: and in thee shall all families of the earth be blessed"* (KJV). Hayward reminds us how this verse played out both during and after WWII:

Hitler had learned that God keeps His threats: "Cursed be everyone who curses you [Israel]." Postwar Germany learned that God also keeps His promises: "Blessed be those who bless you!"[87]

We note from the writings of Grant R. Jeffrey that on May 15, 1948, the leaders of Israel did not fail to remind the world that their nation, above all others, has a distinct connection to the Bible.

---

[85] Alan Hayward, *God's Truth* (Nashville, TN: Thomas Nelson, 1983), 21. See also Genesis 12:3; 27:29; Numbers 24:9.

[86] Ibid., 22.

[87] Ibid.

During hearings before the British Royal Commission on Palestine, David Ben Gurion, as chairman of the Jewish Agency, announced, "The Bible is our only mandate. The mandate of the League [of Nations] is only a recognition of this right and does not establish new things." Remarkably, when the British Mandate over Palestine authorized by the League of Nations, ended at midnight on May 15, 1948, Israel's first prime minister, David Ben Gurion, declared publicly that Israel was once again a nation and now took its rightful place on the stage of world history, Ben Gurion announced, "The Land of Israel was the birthplace of the Jewish people... Here they wrote and gave the Bible to the world... Impelled by this historic association, Jews strove throughout the centuries to go back to the land of their fathers and regain their statehood."[88]

Just as the little baby Moses was marked for death by Pharaoh, so the baby Jesus was marked for death by Herod. Both were protected in infancy by loving parents, and both spent time in Egypt before leaving for their greater victories. Moses took on the mighty Egyptian empire, led his people out of their place of bondage, and prepared them to enter the land God had promised to them to claim as their own.

Following the great victories of Joshua, the land was occupied. The people then fell into many and varied idolatrous practices and virtually abandoned the law that God had given them through Moses. One may wonder how this fragile nation survived. After Solomon's reign, the nation was torn apart. They were pulverized by one empire after another, and at one time they saw the armies of three empires occupy their land at the same time. Both the northern kingdom and the southern domain were forced into exile, with only a few stragglers allowed to remain. They saw two of their temples destroyed, and the third Babylonian deportation was accompanied by the total devastation of their capital city. They were passed around from one empire to the next until their land was finally annexed by the Romans in 63 B.C. After the death of Julius Caesar in 44 B.C., the Romans saw the rise of their first emperor, known to us as Caesar Augustus. Roman soldiers roamed freely throughout the land. Things looked very bleak for the descendants of the people whom Moses had led through the waters of the Red Sea.

[88] Grant R. Jeffrey, *Triumphant Return: The Coming Kingdom of God* (Toronto, ON: Frontier Research Publications, Inc., 2001), 222.

EMMANUEL: GOD WITH US

Hardly anyone noticed, least of all the emperor in far-off Rome, when a little baby made his presence known in the Judean town of Bethlehem. But some did take notice! The shepherds in the fields were made aware of the presence of the promised Messiah by the angel of the Lord, after which they made their way to Bethlehem. As Christians, we never tire of reading the second chapter of Luke, picturing the scene of these humble men standing in awe and wonderment as they gazed upon the baby Jesus and introduced themselves to Mary and Joseph.

Contrary to just about every Christmas pageant ever presented, the king-priests (magi) never saw the baby Jesus in the manger. A careful study of Matthew 2 suggests he was nearly two years old, a toddler in his home, when the wise men from Persia (Iran, or further east) found Him and presented their gifts. Tradition tells us that there were three of them, but all we really know from the Scriptures is they were at least two in number. There could have been twenty or thirty of them, but what we do know is that their visit set off alarm bells in the headquarters of Herod the Great. It did not go unnoticed by this profligate son of depraved humanity that this eastern entourage knew who Jesus was and called Him the King of the Jews. Their travels had been carefully monitored by the Roman authorities, and due to their inquiries, Herod suddenly became a student of Old Testament prophetic Scripture, wanting to know all about the Jewish Messiah. He had murdered some of his own family members to secure his position and was now a puppet king for Rome in Judaea. He wanted no other kings, including the baby Jesus, in his domain.

According to Matthew 2:16, the departure of the wise men unleashed a bloodbath in which Herod had every male child aged two years and under put to death in and around Bethlehem. Like Pharaoh of old in the time of Moses, he carried out his cruel enterprise with efficiency. Mary and Joseph escaped to Egypt, where they would have seen the same pyramids we marvel at today, returning home only after the death of Herod.

TWELVE CHOSEN MEN

The stage is now set for the Lord Jesus and his twelve disciples to make their appearance in history. The officials of Rome took scant notice when a man called Jesus Christ was crucified at a time when many thousands suffered the same fate, but their interest was aroused when the teachings of Jesus were carried throughout the far reaches of the mightiest empire the world had ever seen. The early Christians, with their message of redemption for mankind, challenged every religious system and idolatrous practice of Rome, refusing to worship the emperor. They were armed only with the Old Testament Scriptures (which included the writings of Moses) and the power of the Holy Spirit. No other writings have ever had such an impact on the world. The power of Rome collapsed under its own weight while the church continues to thrive to our present day.

CHAPTER SEVEN

Is the Bible Reliable?

We have also a more sure word of prophecy; whereunto ye do well that ye take heed, as unto a light that shineth in a dark place, until the day dawn, and the day star arise in your hearts: knowing this first, that no prophecy of the scripture is of any private interpretation. For the prophecy came not in old time by the will of man: but holy men of God spake as they were moved by the Holy Ghost. (2 Peter 1:19–21, KJV)

A PERSONAL TESTIMONY

My early interest in the Bible was greatly enhanced by the influence of two wonderful people. One was my paternal grandmother, Freda Mersereau, in whose large and spacious house I spent many happy hours. She was an avid reader who prized good books, especially the Bible. The other was Florence Alexander, my Sunday school teacher at the Baptist church in Fredericton Junction, New Brunswick. At my request, she procured for me one of the old pew Bibles from our church. I still remember its well-worn pages and its heavy black cover.

I sat down one Sunday afternoon with this Bible and read the entire book of Genesis. I found the first few chapters a difficult read. I didn't know what a firmament was; I couldn't figure out how people lived so long in those days. By the time I got to Abraham, it got more interesting, but I was especially fascinated with Joseph, whose life story covers a large part of the first book of the Bible. To this day, Genesis is among my favourite books and Joseph is my favourite Bible character.

On another occasion, shortly thereafter, I picked up my father's Bible, and while thumbing through its pages I came upon Revelation and began to read. I found myself in a strange world come to life with a host of sights and sounds, with water everywhere and beasts coming out of nowhere. There was a horrifying burning lake of fire and, finally, a beautiful city with streets of gold. I didn't know when these events would take place. I read the entire book in one sitting. I still struggle with the last book of the Bible, but I am blessed every time I read it.

As you can see, my early experience with the Bible saw me getting acquainted with the bookends (Genesis and Revelation), but the sixty-four books in between were still to be explored. My initial acquaintance with the Scriptures came as a young child in Sunday school, but I was in junior high before I began to read the Bible with any degree of seriousness. I am convinced that my reading of the first and last books of the Bible at the age of fourteen was a contributing factor in my conversion two years later at the Leighton Ford crusade in Fredericton, New Brunswick.

The days following my salvation were exciting but also challenging. My parents had rededicated their lives to the Lord at the same crusade meetings in which I had come to Christ, and my brother came to faith shortly afterward. I became acquainted with Pastor Norwood Brawn at the Peoples Church in Fredericton, who soon became the teacher of a weekly ladies Bible class held in my home area. Wanting to become better-versed in the Scriptures, I began attending this class, where Pastor Brawn's teaching gave me the foundational truths that put me on the road to Bible School training and pastoral ministry.

Before my conversion, I had been attending the local Baptist church in my community, but I soon learned that neither my pastor nor my church family had any enthusiasm for my salvation experience. It soon became clear to me that, though this man held several degrees from a well-known Baptist university in Nova Scotia, he was a stranger to grace and held a very skeptical view of the authority and veracity of the Bible. It came as a great shock to me when he suggested that salvation was a matter of personal opinion, and he did what he could to dampen my joy and excitement. It was my first experience with the liberal theology that raged through many theological schools in the 1940s and 50s. I am glad to say that this pastor came to faith a year before his sudden passing in 1967.

I had naively believed in my early Christian life that all pastors were Christians and that all churches embraced the truth of the Bible. I was jolted into reality when I realized that such was not the case. In our own day, evangelicalism is increasingly challenged in the area of biblical authority, and many no longer accept the biblical account of creation or the catastrophic flood of Genesis. There is also skepticism about everlasting punishment in hell, a subject that is rarely addressed from our pulpits today.

CLARITY VS. CHAOS

These are days of confusion and chaos in our society, as well as in our churches. Christians have been affected by a culture that is increasingly prone to reject anything that remotely resembles absolute truth. The Bible is treated lightly and its teachings considered antiquated and out of touch with our modern world. These ominous words from Erwin Lutzer tell us of the challenge we face:

> Obviously dark days lie ahead for the believing church since Christianity is no longer providing the consensus for our society. The freedoms Christianity brought to us are being destroyed before our eyes. We are living at a time when humanistic thinking is coming to its natural conclusions in morals, education, and law. If we are to withstand the onslaught, we must be convinced in our minds that we have a message from God, a sure word that "shines in a dark place."[89]

Even within evangelical circles, the inerrancy of Scripture has been a hotly debated issue. Harold Lindsell has written, without apology, that the issue of honesty is what is really at stake here. He offers this challenge to any institution or organization that provides an umbrella for a mixed multitude with a variety of opposing views on this important topic:

> How is it that when errancy begins to creep in among evangelicals it always is accompanied by ethical deceit and moral failure?... How is it possible for evangelical schools that are controlled by orthodox doctrinal statements knowingly to permit members of their faculties to teach what is contrary to their confessional commitments? How is it possible for faculty members of seminaries to sign doctrinal statements as though they believed what they signed, but to do it tongue-in-cheek? How is

---

[89] Kroll, *Back to the Bible*, 129.

it possible for evangelical schools to keep on telling their constituencies that they really are evangelical with regard to Scripture when they know they are not? Why don't institutions that have abandoned inerrancy in Principle say so in such a way that people everywhere know this to be true? Why soft-pedal the change in position and pussyfoot around the issue? Among denominations, why do men who dissent from their confessions of faith remain within those denominations with the intention of subverting others? Would not honesty and integrity lead them to dissociate themselves from these denominations and go where they could honestly agree with the doctrinal commitments or at least to places where there are no doctrinal commitments?[90]

This is a time for all Christians to open their eyes. Under the broad and ever-widening label of evangelicalism many of our most influential leaders have made, and continue to make, major concessions in the area of biblical authority. Many no longer accept the historicity of the first eleven chapters of Genesis, and to compound the difficulty, some have adopted some form of theistic evolution. The Petrine authorship of 2 Peter is fully denied, even though the letter itself claims otherwise and the Pauline authorship of Ephesians is rejected in spite of the internal evidence to the contrary. Jonah is treated like any fictional tale from which we can learn some practical lessons, while its historical authenticity is denied.

It is nothing short of incredible that today's average evangelical Christian remains silent while leaders on the cutting edge of contemporary Christianity prove by their words and actions that their view of the Scriptures is on the low end of the scale. Hear what Brian McLaren has to say about Christianity in relation to other religious systems:

I don't believe making disciples must equal making adherents to the Christian religion… it may be advisable in many (not all!) circumstances to help people become followers of Jesus and remain within their Buddhist, Hindu, or Jewish contexts.[91]

This surely runs counter to the Word of God, which admonishes us to remain separate from associations that could potentially weaken and/or compromise our Christian witness. Paul urges us in 2 Corinthians 6:14–18 not to lock ourselves

[90] Lindsell, *The Battle for the Bible*, 207.
[91] MacArthur, *The Truth War*, 34.

into relationships that could force us into divided loyalties. Paul does not mean we must live in isolation from all unbelievers; he encourages Christians to stay with their unbelieving spouses (2 Corinthians 5:9–10; 7:12–13).

A believer is not to enter into marriage with a nonbeliever. More than that, Christians are cautioned not to affiliate with religious systems not based on the Bible. From ancient times, Babylon was portrayed as a city of luxury, immorality, adultery, and false religion. This can all be tracked to the Tower of Babel in Genesis 11:1–9. Vividly described in Revelation 17–18, God's voice from heaven is crisp and clear regarding Babylon: *"Come out of her, my people"* (Revelation 18:4, KJV).

The early Christians formed their own assemblies and abandoned their temples of idol worship. They often met in Jewish synagogues for worship, but there was no attempt to form an alliance with the Jewish religious system.

Tony Campolo, who has had such a positive ministry with young people, has a very negative take on Scripture, evidenced by his statement to a reporter explaining why he wrote the book *Speaking My Mind*.[92] Campolo raised more questions then he answered by asking, "When did evangelical Christianity become anti-gay… When did it become so negative towards other religious groups?"[93] One of the more popular preachers in America today causes us to wince when he says his readers should "challenge and question Christian doctrines (like the virgin birth and the Trinity)… He also says that verses in the Bible aren't first and foremost timeless truths."[94] Well-known scholar Bernard Ramm appears to contradict all that he has ever taught concerning the inerrancy of Scripture when "he limits the Bible-only principle to matters of faith and conduct… he says that every page of the Bible is crowded with a cluster of problems."[95]

AUGUSTINE

How very different is the view of Augustine, the fourth-century theologian and noted scholar. Many have faulted this North African church leader for his allegorical approach to Scripture, especially the book of Revelation. His prolific writings dealt with such important issues as the Trinity, predestination, the nature of evil, and free will. His writings were read voraciously by Martin Luther, who became the driving force behind the Reformation movement in the sixteenth

---

[92] Tony Campolo, *Speaking My Mind* (Nashville, TN: W Publishing Group/Thomas Nelson, 2004).
[93] MacArthur, *The Truth War*, 139.
[94] John Piper and Justin Taylor, *The Supremacy of Christ in a Postmodern World* (Wheaton, IL: Crossway Books, 2007), 134.
[95] Lindsell, *The Bible in the Balance*, 48.

century. Among Augustine's early writings are those dealing with the authority of Scripture, and it can be seen that he held a high view of God's Word. Here is an excerpt from Harold Lindsell's book, *The Battle for the Bible*, as insight is given into Augustine's thoughts on the authority of Scripture:

> Of all the church fathers none, perhaps, attained the stature that Augustine reached in his age and in the long history of the Christian church since then. Surely no other early church father had more influence on the life of Calvin and through him on the Reformed churches of the Reformation. His attitude toward the Scriptures should bear weight, especially among those in the Reformed tradition. He said, "The Faith will totter if the authority of the Holy Scriptures loses its hold on men. We must surrender ourselves to the authority of Holy Scripture, for it can neither mislead nor be misled."
>
> "The question," says [George Duncan Barry[96]]… "'Why Christ Himself did not write any Book' is answered by Augustine in these remarkable words. 'His members gave out the knowledge which they had received *through the dictation of the Head*; whatever He willed us to read concerning His own words and acts, He bade them write, as *though they were His very own* words.' More unguardedly still, Augustine teaches that we see in the Gospels the very Hand of the Lord which He wore in His own Body… There are no contradictions of each other's writings in the Books of the Four Evangelists. 'We must demonstrate that the Four Sacred writers are not at variance with each other. For our opponents… frequently maintain that discrepancies are found in the Evangelists.'… Freely do I admit to you, my friend, that I have learnt to ascribe to those Books which are of Canonical rank, and only to them, such reverence and honour that I firmly believe that no single error due to the author is found in any one of them. And when I am confronted in these Books with anything that seems to be at variance with truth, I do not hesitate to put it down either to the use of an incorrect text, or to the failure of a commentator rightly to explain the words, or to my own mistaken understanding of the passage."[97]

---

[96] Quoted from George Duncan Barry, *The Inspiration and Authority of Holy Scriptures, A Study in the Literature of the First Five Centuries* (New York, NY: Macmillan, 1919), 10.

[97] Lindsell, *The Battle for the Bible*, 53–54.

WHO MOVED THE STONE?

Howard Hendricks tells us the fascinating story of Frank Morison (the pen name for Albert Henry Ross), the British journalist who in the early part of the twentieth century mounted a detailed study of the Scriptures in order to disprove the resurrection of Jesus Christ. Greatly influenced by certain scholars who discounted all miracles and viewed the world as being governed by natural law and forces, Morison determined to find out why the followers of Jesus unanimously agreed that Jesus had risen from the dead. He studied every detail of the seven days leading up to Christ's crucifixion. Going through the four Gospels, he examined the lives of each of the apostles, giving special attention to Peter the fisherman and James, the brother of the Lord Jesus. He also studied the life of the apostle Paul in full detail, including his remarkable conversion and his convictions related to the resurrection. Special attention was also given to the trial of Jesus before Jewish officials and Pilate, the Roman governor. Since the resurrection is, without doubt, the most astounding miracle in the Bible, Morison reasoned that disproving such would severely damage the credibility of the Bible.[98]

The carefully documented material gathered by this British investigator was to provide the foundational elements for a book he had planned to write to prove that the Bible was subject to error and deception. With the greatest of miracles debunked (the resurrection), all of Christianity would then be seen as fraudulent and unworthy of any serious consideration. This became the book that refused to be written, as Morison found what he was *not* looking for—namely, irrefutable proof that the resurrection was a fact rooted not only in the Bible, but in history. His investigation led him to embrace the truth of the resurrection and acknowledge faith in the Lord Jesus Christ, resulting in his conversion to Christianity. In 1930, Frank Morison published *Who Moved the Stone?*, one of the most powerful defences of the resurrection of Christ ever to be put into print.

The child of God can confidently trust the Word of God to be fully accurate, whether it speaks of science, history, geography, or chronology. The spade of the archaeologist has proven to be an enduring ally of biblical truth, and while the Bible needs no external proofs to verify its claims, it is heartening to know that not one of its claims has ever been disproved by archaeological discovery.

There have been increasing attacks on the Scriptures, starting in the days of Darwin in the nineteenth century and on into the twentieth century as theologians emerged who were increasingly skeptical of the reliability of the

---

[98] Howard G. Hendricks and William D. Hendricks, *Living by the Book: The Art and Science of Reading the Bible* (Chicago, IL: Moody Publishers, 2007), 80–82.

Bible. Whole schools of theology succumbed to a more liberal influence that crossed all denominational lines and affected many ministers and their churches.

WAS MOSES ABLE TO WRITE?

The most virulent attacks on the Word of God have usually been concentrated on the books of Genesis, Exodus, Leviticus, Numbers, and Deuteronomy, usually referred to as the books of Moses. W.A. Criswell has stated that "the book of Genesis has been considered a hopeless collection of unsubstantiated myths."[99] Modern criticism has made some bold claims that have since been disproved. It was once thought that Moses could not have penned any writings of the Bible because writing had not been invented in his time. Discoveries have since proved that writing was a well-established art in the Near East many centuries before the time of Moses.

> Instead of writing being unknown in the days of Moses, we have discovered that centuries and centuries before the time of Moses writing was a most extended, well-developed art, far antedating the time of the great lawgiver.[100]

The campaign of the kings in Genesis 14 has been fully substantiated by archaeological discovery. At one time the home city of Abraham, Ur of the Chaldees, was treated in the same fairy-tale fashion as the Land of Oz of Hollywood fame, but now we can walk through the wide streets that were so familiar to Abraham since much of the city has been uncovered. This vast ancient metropolis had its own sanitation system, beautiful homes with spacious patios, and tall decorated columns. Criswell notes, "As an added touch the name itself 'Abram' has been found inscribed on some of the columns in the ancient city."[101]

THE HITTITES: FACT OF FICTION?

As the twentieth century dawned on the human race, critics increasingly scoffed at the biblical account of the Hittites (mentioned over fifty times in the Bible), suggesting that no such people ever existed. All that has changed thanks to what Criswell refers to as the "miner prophets" of modern times, the archaeologists.[102] A large Hittite library has been found in modern Turkey, and some of their

---

[99] Criswell, *Why I Preach*, 51.
[100] Ibid., 51–52.
[101] Ibid., 52.
[102] Ibid., 54.

principal cities have been excavated. Their vast empire rivalled that of Egypt and Assyria.[103]

> It is now known that the Hittites were in possession of advanced technological processes for smelting iron for all commercial purposes. They were renowned horsemen and were the first to manufacture chariots with iron fittings and use them as weapons of war. From the extant Royal Addresses it is evident that the ancient Hittites valued the arts of peace also, for the texts indicate that they had already enjoyed a prolonged tradition of settled court life… The inviolability of oaths, covenants, and treaties was consistently emphasized, as in other ancient Near Eastern systems of jurisprudence; but in contrast to the codes of Hammurabi and Moses, the principle of retaliation was subordinate to that of restitution. One additional feature of Hittite legislative and social enlightenment can be seen in the marked degree of respect and accord to women.[104]

Hittite roots can be traced to the days of Abraham, extending into the days of Solomon, when their distinct identity was lost.[105]

According to Genesis 23, Abraham purchased the cave of Machpelah from Ephron the Hittite as a burial site for his wife, Sarah. Esau married two Hittite women to the great disappointment of his parents (Genesis 26:34–35; 27:46). One of David's faithful generals was Uriah the Hittite. The Hittites trace their ancestry to Ham, the son of Noah, through Canaan's second son, Heth (Genesis 10:15; 1 Chronicles 1:13).

AHAB AND JEZEBEL: TRUTH OUT OF THE EARTH (PSALM 85:11)

Much humour has been made of not only the debauched character of Jezebel but whether such a woman ever existed. According to the Scriptures, this Sidonian princess became the wife of Ahab, who ruled the northern kingdom of Israel for twenty-two years in the early part of the ninth century B.C. Her life is detailed from 1 Kings 16:31 to the end of 2 Kings 9. She is revealed as a vain, strong-willed idolatrous queen who contributed to the ruination of her husband's royal line and the weakening of the kingdom that capitulated to the Assyrians in the next century.

---

[103] Tenney, *Zondervan's Pictorial Bible Dictionary*, 356.

[104] R.K. Harrison, *Introduction to the Old Testament* (Grand Rapids: Eerdmans, 1973), 117.

[105] Douglas, ed., "The Hittites of Canann," *The New Bible Dictionary*, 476–477.

The story of Ahab, the seventh king of Israel, occupies the last six chapters of 1 Kings in contrast to his famous father, Omri, whose reign is covered in just thirteen verses (1 Kings 16:16–28). In addition to the ambitious and continuing building program inherited from his father on the three-hundred-foot outcropping called the mountain of Samaria (1 Kings 16:24), Ahab erected a massive royal palace known as the house of ivory (1 Kings 22:39). Prior to excavations of the old city of Samaria,[106] numerous scholars had determined that the house of ivory was an absurdity inserted into the text by an overly zealous writer. In the early decades of the twentieth century, however, excavations of the hill of Samaria revealed the very opposite.

> The foundations of Israel's capital rests on virgin soil, Omri had in fact acquired new land… this otherwise peaceful and lonely hill must have been one great bustling building site… the walls are fifteen feet thick.[107]

The removal of the rubble revealed shards and splinters of ivory that seemed to be present everywhere over the many acres of land.

Werner Keller gives this observation:

> There was only one explanation of these finds: this place was the famous "ivory house" of King Ahab… this monarch did not build his entire palace of ivory… it is now quite clear what happened: Ahab had the rooms of the palace decorated with this wonderful material and filled them with ivory furniture.[108]

The assumption by some that the entire building was made wholly of ivory is probably what fuelled speculation as to the veracity of the account.

Ahab and Jezebel's most infamous act was the murder of Naboth, their next-door neighbour, and the annexing of his vineyard in the northern district of Jezreel to the royal estate. The vivid details are given to us in 1 Kings 21. Their treachery incurred the judgment of God, whose displeasure brought about their violent and bloody deaths as well as the almost total extermination of their posterity and the end of Ahab's family rule in the northern kingdom. All of this was prophesied by the prophet Elijah (1 Kings 21:20–24).

---

[106] The hill, the city, and the region were all called Samaria.
[107] Werner Keller, The Bible as History, trans. William Neil (New York, NY: William Morrow and Company, 1963), 232.
[108] Ibid., 233.

The incident of Naboth's vineyard is evident testimony of the powerful influence of Jezebel in the northern kingdom. The city of Jezreel was located twenty-five miles north of Samaria and was the site of another of Ahab's royal palaces, the primary residence of Ahab and Jezebel. The city takes its name from

> the entire valley of Jezreel that separates Galilee from Samaria including the valley of Esdraelon (Megiddo). The valley was important militarily as a battle site for Deborah (Judges 4–5), Gideon (Judg. 6-7), Saul (2 Sam. 4), Jehu (2 Kings 9–10), and Josiah (2 Kings 22).[109]

Jezebel did not recognize the covenant relationship between Yahveh (Jehovah) and the people of Israel. Seeing her weak husband in a pout over his failure to persuade Naboth to sell his land, she took matters into her own hands. Usurping the authority of her husband and accessing the use of his seal, she had Naboth falsely accused and subsequently murdered along with his sons (1 Kings 21:4–14; 2 Kings 9:26).

Ahab's possession of Naboth's vineyard was met with a personal visit from Elijah, who declared, *"Thus saith the Lord, In the place where dogs licked the blood of Naboth shall dogs lick thy blood, even thine"* (1 Kings 21:19, KJV). Although questioned by some, this prophecy was fulfilled at least representatively when the body of Ahab's son, Joram, was thrown to the dogs in Naboth's vineyard (2 Kings 9:25–26). Some suggest that the full impact of this utterance was at least partly thwarted by the seeming repentance of Ahab in response to Elijah's stern warning (1 Kings 21:27–29). The full impact of God's judgment was delayed until after Ahab was off the scene.

Following his third military campaign against Aram, the mortally wounded Ahab was taken to the capital city of Samaria in his blood-splattered chariot, where he died from his wounds (1 Kings 22). Ahab's death brought their older son, Ahaziah, to the throne. He died in his palace in Samaria during the second year of his reign as the result of a severe fall. Since he left no male heirs, the northern kingdom passed to his younger brother Jehoram (Joram), who reigned for twelve years. In the meantime, Ahab and Jezebel's daughter, Athaliah, married Jehoram the son of Jehoshaphat, king of Judah. Just as Omri, the king of Israel, had years before arranged the marriage of his son Ahab to Jezebel, so Jehoshaphat, for political advantage, arranged the marriage of his son to the northern princess, Athaliah (2 Kings 8:18; 2 Chronicles 18:1).

[109] Charles W. Draper, Chad Brand, and Archie England, eds., "Jezreel," *Holman Illustrated Bible Dictionary* (Nashville, TN: Holman Bible Publishers, 2003), 922.

This material from Omer J. Hancock will greatly assist the reader at this juncture:

> Joram—Personal name meaning "Yahweh is exalted." Name of a king of Israel (849–843 BC) and a king of Judah (850–843 BC). The possibility of confusion between them is aggravated by several factors. For one thing, both are also called Jehoram. For another, they were contemporary with one another. Finally, each reigned in proximity to a person named Ahaziah: Joram of Judah was succeeded on the throne by his son, whose name was Ahaziah; Joram of Israel came to the throne at the death of his brother, who was also named Ahaziah. The account of the reign of Joram (Jehoram of Israel) is found in 2 Kings 3. He led a coalition with Judah and Edom, advised by Elisha, to defeat Moab. The reign of Joram of Judah is treated in 2 Kings 8. He married the daughter of Ahab of Israel [Athaliah] and brought Baal worship to Judah. Edom and Libnah gained independence from Judah in his reign.[110]

Jehoram's ascension to the throne following his father's death was initiated by the murdering of his six brothers (2 Chronicles 21:1–5). After an eight-year rule, he died from a loathsome disease, leaving his son Ahaziah to ascend the throne of Judah. This is where the account can become very complicated for even the most astute student of the Scriptures.[111] Ahaziah's uncle, whose name was Jehu, son of Jehoshaphat, had been promised the throne of Israel by the prophet Elisha, who also informed Jehu that he would be God's instrument to punish Ahab's household for his sins and the sins of Jezebel. Ahaziah (king of Judah and grandson of Jezebel) went to the district of Jezreel, the location of Naboth's vineyard, to visit Jehoram (Ahaziah's uncle and Jezebel's son), who was convalescing from wounds received in battle with the Arameans.

With many of the fighting men tied up with the defence of Ramoth-gilead, Jehu hastened to the palace estate and waited in Naboth's vineyard for the arrival of Ahaziah and Jehoram. As the two kings approached the soon-to-be king of Israel, they realized he was not alone. Jehu was accompanied by officers who were carefully chosen and well-positioned to bait his two guests into a trap from which there would be no escape. Jehoram was alerted to their dire predicament when Jehu dismissed any kind of peace proposal so long as the witchcraft and immorality of Jezebel was tolerated in the royal household. Shouting a warning

---

[110] Ibid., 945–946.

[111] A reading of 2 Kings 9 will greatly assist the serious student of the Bible at this point.

to Ahaziah, Jehoram (Jezebel's son) bolted for safety but was soon struck down by a well-placed arrow from the bow of Jehu.[112]

This was the beginning of the end of the dynasty of Omri, as well as the family influence of King Ahab in the northern kingdom. The king of Judah attempted his own escape from the clutches of Jehu, but was soon surrounded by Jehu's men and assassinated. With the two kings eliminated, Jehu made a dash for the main gate of the palace precinct, where he fully expected to encounter yet another challenge to his claim on the throne.

Having heard of her son Ahaziah's death, Athaliah assumed the throne of Judah with seemingly little resistance. With a cold and vicious callousness that typified her mother, Jezebel, she murdered her own grandchildren so as to negate any possible future threat to her royal position (2 Kings 11:1). Only one of her descendants escaped her bloody purge, an infant by the name of Joash, who was secreted to the temple, where he remained protected by Jehoida, the high priest (2 Chronicles 22:11–12). Six years later, in the face of strong protests from Athaliah, Joash was crowned king of the southern kingdom (2 Chronicles 23:11). As she exited the temple compound following his coronation, she was executed by the royal guard (2 Kings 11:13–15).[113]

With her son and grandson both swept off the scene, Jezebel's political fortunes were in total disarray.

One writer observes,

After Ahab's death, Jezebel continued as a power in Israel for 10 years, in her role as a queen-mother, throughout the reign of Ahaziah, then during Jehoram's lifetime. When Jehoram was killed by Jehu she attired herself regally (2 Ki. 9:30), and awaited him. She mocked Jehu, and went to her fate with courage and dignity (842 BC).[114]

Threading her way through the labyrinthine hallways of the palace that had been her home for most of her adult life, she came to a high window that gave her an unobstructed view of the main gate. From that same window, she could also view the huge piece of real estate that had belonged to the man called Naboth (before she and her husband had falsely accused and murdered him in order to confiscate his property). Driving his chariot at breakneck speed, Jehu

[112] T.A. Bryant, comp., "Jehu," *Today's Dictionary of the Bible* (Minneapolis: Bethany House, 1982), 331–332.
[113] Ibid., "Athaliah," 64–65.
[114] Douglas, ed., "Jezebel," *The New Bible Dictionary*, 587.

came into view and approached the gate to lay claim to the royal title for which he had been anointed by the messenger of Elisha (2 Kings 9:6). Ignoring the verbal taunts of the lady in the window, he ordered some nearby officials to throw her to the ground.

Curious onlookers must have been gripped with utter horror and dismay as Jezebel, thrashing wildly and spitting obscenities, smashed against the wall as she was hurled to the ground, trampled beyond recognition under Jehu's chariot wheels.

The gathering crowd knew this was the end for Jezebel. Now the woman who had persecuted and killed hundreds of God's people was just a battered and crumpled corpse. Even the prophet Elijah, fearful for his life, had temporarily suspended his public ministry and fled for refuge to the wilderness. Bringing her idolatrous practices from Tyre and Sidon, Jezebel had made every effort to discourage all worship of Jehovah. Using every manipulative technique possible, including cold-blooded murder, she used her weak-kneed husband for her own evil designs. Dabbling in every form of witchcraft and immorality, she had turned the royal palace into a Peyton Place for every kind of moral deviant and social outcast.[115]

As the chariots of Jehu and his men clattered their way into the palace compound, where they celebrated their victory with feasting and drinking, the body of Jezebel was savaged by wild dogs who carried off her legs and torso, leaving behind her skull, hands, and feet (2 Kings 9:33–37).

But what of the skeptics who at one time considered Jezebel and the events surrounding her life as nothing more than a fanciful tale with little historical evidence to verify its authenticity? What of those who suggested that the Sidonian princess herself was a fictional character injected into the account to give added interest and excitement to a largely fictional tale?

Historical investigation, supported by archaeological discovery, has greatly increased our pool of information about the events surrounding the reign of Ahab in the northern kingdom. We also know conclusively that there is far more substance to Jezebel's place in history than was previously believed.

Twenty-eight centuries following the showdown between Jehu and Jezebel at the gate of Jezreel, historians were prompted to a renewed interest in the northern kingdom of Israel (Samaria). Poking around the ancient ruins of King Ahab's palace grounds and the surrounding area, twentieth-century archaeologists uncovered a beautifully crafted signet ring (or seal) buried deeply in the earth.

---

[115] Tenney, "Jezebel," *Zondervan's Pictorial Bible Dictionary*, 431.

Though ravaged by corrosion, its design was dated to the timeframe of King Ahab, and engraved on the ring was a name that was still legible after nearly three thousand years—"Jezebel."[116] We now know that Jezebel was indeed able to act in an official capacity, exercising her full authority.

This discovery not only silences the critics who question her authenticity as an historical personage, it also bears witness to how powerful an influence she exerted following her marriage to Ahab. A seal or signet is a device that bears a name or design that can be imparted to a soft substance such as clay or wax. Their use goes back thousands of years, and they were prominent throughout the civilized world. They were usually made of limestone, metal, or precious stones. Many of these signet rings were made by a professional seal-cutter whose work was fine-tuned by the use of a cutting wheel or pin of iron with a point of a diamond (Jeremiah 17:1).[117] Some were carried around the neck or waist, and others were carried in a box. The majority were made into finger rings and carried the name of the owner. Many Hebrew seals have been found, bearing such names as Hananiah, Menahem, Micaiah, Jotham, Nehemiah, Gedaliah, and Azariah. A seal with the name of the owner carried the full weight and authority of that person.[118]

Was Jezebel wearing her ring when she took her precipitous fall from an upper balcony to the ground below and under the wheels of Jehu's chariot? Was it taken from her corpse by an enterprising scavenger who dropped it in the aftermath of Jehu's entry into the palace grounds? Or was it perhaps taken south to the city of Samaria later, following the death of Jezebel? Was it thrown by the former queen in defiance at Jehu and his men as they prepared to occupy the royal territory of Samaria? Was it taken from her private apartments in either Jezreel or Samaria by a curious official, from which it became lost in antiquity? Was it picked up by one of Jehu's men and deposited in places unknown?

We do not know where this seal was lost or who last handled it before it was buried for many centuries. But we do know that this signet ring was once worn by a person who is fully authenticated as the wife of King Ahab in northern Israel and whose legacy still survives in the archives of all that is infamous in the annals of ancient history.

HANDWRITING ON THE WALL

Have you ever heard the expression "the writing is on the wall"? This comes straight out of the fifth chapter of Daniel, where Belshazzar the king hosted a great

---

[116] Henry Morris, *The Henry Morris Study Bible* (Green Forest, AR: Master Books, 2012), 572.
[117] Douglas, ed., "Seal," *The New Bible Dictionary*, 1070–1071.
[118] Tenney, "Seal," *Zondervan's Pictorial Bible Dictionary*, 764–765.

feast for his chief officers and the prominent citizens of the city of Babylon. They were drinking wine from drinking vessels that Nebuchadnezzar had taken from the temple in Jerusalem many years earlier. In this atmosphere of merrymaking and drunkenness, a man's hand suddenly appeared in clear view of Belshazzar, who was gripped with fear as the fingers wrote a message on the wall.

Unable to decipher the message, he called for the wise men of Babylon, but they were perplexed by the strange language and admitted to the king their inability to read or interpret it. With encouragement from the queen (possibly the queen mother), the aged Daniel was called to the scene. It is obvious from the context that Belshazzar was in a drunken state, for he belittled Daniel as being one of the exiles from Jerusalem. However, the throng of people was immediately brought to silence as Daniel revealed the message.

Before revealing it, Daniel reminded Belshazzar of how Nebuchadnezzar had learned of the sovereignty of God over the nations. He further revealed that Belshazzar had not acknowledged the one true God, as did his grandfather, and therefore he merited the judgment of God. Daniel tells Belshazzar in a few short words where he has gone off track: *"But the God in whose hand are your life-breath and all your ways, you have not glorified"* (Daniel 5:23, NASB), and then he sums up the meaning of the writing:

> *God has numbered the days of your kingdom and brought it to an end… you have been weighed in the balance and found deficient… your kingdom has been divided and given to the Medes and Persians.* (Daniel 5:26–28, HCSB)

Daniel read and interpreted the writing… Mene, Mene, Tekel, and Parsin. The words are clearly Aramaic and form a sequence of weights, decreasing from a mina, to a shekel ($1/60^{th}$ of a mina), to a half shekel. It was not that the king and wise men could not read them, but they failed to understand their significance for Belshazzar. Read as verbs (with different vowels attached to the Aramaic consonants), the sequence becomes: "Numbered, numbered, weighed, and divided" The Lord had numbered the days of Belshazzar's kingdom and brought it to an end because he had been weighed in the balance and found wanting (v. 27). The repetition of "numbered" may suggest that it will occur quickly.[119]

[119] *ESV Study Bible* (Wheaton, IL: Crossway Bibles, 2008), 1596.

Before the night was over, Belshazzar was dead and his kingdom was conquered by the Medes and the Persians (Daniel 5:30).

The critics have had a field day with the book of Daniel and for many years boasted that the man called Belshazzar never existed. The spade of the archaeologist, however, has silenced the skeptics and provided an abundance of documented evidence for his existence. Not only do we know that he was coregent with his father, Nabonidus, during the days of Daniel, but he was also one of the most significant leaders of that period. Excavations in and around the city of Babylon have given us the names of his secretaries and yielded the names of his sisters.[120]

The ancient secular histories, along with discoveries made in more recent times by archaeologists, have combined to fully verify the events of the fifth chapter of Daniel. As Belshazzar shook in fear while the handwriting appeared on the wall, the Medes and Persians led by Cyrus were at that very moment diverting the flow of the Euphrates river, allowing them to march on the dry riverbed under the massive walls of Babylon and into the city. Before the attendants had time to clear the tables at Belshazzar's well-attended banquet, the city was overrun by the enemy.

The Chaldean king and his guests continued the party late into the night. Cyrus and his Persian forces were even then entering the city with full intent on crashing Belshazzar's party. Perhaps Cyrus knew through spies sent beforehand, or through insiders willing to betray their city for a price, that this was the right time to attack the unsuspecting Chaldeans. Cyrus may have had a week or more to break into the city, since these parties sometimes lasted for many days. The thousands of people drinking themselves into a drunken frenzy were in no shape to offer any real resistance to the Persian invaders. While many in the city went to sleep under Chaldean rule, they woke up under the rule of Cyrus the Persian.

Ralph Woodrow comments,

Learning of a great pagan festival that the Babylonians would be observing, Cyrus planned a surprise attack. On the night of the festival— when the inhabitants and king would be spending their time in revelry and drunkenness—he would channel the waters of the Euphrates (which ran beneath the walls and through the city) into a 40 square mile area which had been built for flood control. This being accomplished with

---

[120] Criswell, *Why I Preach*, 55.

the lowering of the water, the armies of Cyrus would march through the river bed and beneath the outer wall![121]

The armies of Cyrus managed to penetrate the outer walls, but the inner walls with the massive brass gates, which were usually closed and locked, would be a formidable barrier to entering the city proper.

But in the neglect and spell of the celebrations, these gates had not been shut! *Now we can understand the significance of the words: "Thus saith the Lord... to Cyrus... I will open before him the two leaved gates: and* the gates shall not be shut... *I will break in pieces the gates of brass and cut in sunder the bars of iron"* (Isaiah 45:1–2).[122]

This incredible prophecy, made one hundred fifty years before the time of Cyrus, assured the Persian king that God would open the way for him to conquer the heavily fortified city of Babylon. The armies of Cyrus had free access to the city because God had gone before them in answer to Isaiah's amazing prophecy. Cyrus entered the city less than three weeks later, where he was cordially received by the citizens as well as their Jewish captives.

According to the *Nabonidus Chronicle,* Babylon fell to the Medo-Persians on the sixteenth of the month Tishri, in the autumn of 539 B.C. The Greek historians and Xenophon supply fascinating details about Babylon's fall. The *Nabonidus Chronicle* and the Cyrus Cylinder both agree with Daniel that Babylon was captured without a major battle and the citizens readily accepted Persian rule (6:1–3).[123]

According to Josephus, once Cyrus entered the city of Babylon he consulted with the Jewish populace, who in turn introduced him to their Scriptures. He especially noted the seventy-year captivity found in the writings of Jeremiah 25:1–14 and 29:10–14. Cyrus read with great interest that the Jews were to be freed after the seventy-year exile and permitted to return to their own land and the city of Jerusalem. Cyrus knew that he had just defeated the nation (Babylon) that had taken the Jews into exile, and that nearly seventy years had already

---

[121] Ralph Woodrow, *Great Prophecies of the Bible* (Palm Springs, CA: Ralph Woodrow Evangelistic Association, 1989), 90–91.

[122] Ibid., 91.

[123] *The Apologetics Study Bible* (Nashville, TN: Holman Bible Publishers, 2007), 1279.

passed since their deportation. Excitement was in the air as Cyrus and some of the Jewish scholars scanned the book of Isaiah, especially Isaiah 44 and 45.[124]

There before his eyes was his own name in Isaiah 44:28:

> One special point of interest is that Cyrus read his own name in the book of Isaiah. Knowing this was written 140 years before the temple was destroyed, and now another 70 years had also passed, he was stirred to action! In the first year of the reign of Cyrus, which was the seventieth from the day that our people were removed out of their own land into Babylon… that after they had undergone that servitude seventy years, he would restore them again to the land of their fathers, and they should build their temple… God stirred up the mind of Cyrus, and made him write this throughout all Asia: "Thus saith Cyrus… indeed foretold my name by the prophets, and that I should build him a house at Jerusalem." This was known to Cyrus by his reading the book which Isaiah left behind him of his prophecies… *one hundred and forty years before the temple was demolished*… an earnest desire and ambition seized upon him to fulfil what was so written.[125]

The official document that Cyrus drew up and signed to permit the Jews to return to their land is found in the pages of Holy Writ (Ezra 1:1–3; 2 Chronicles 36:22–23). Note especially Ezra 1:2:

> *This is what King Cyrus of Persia says: "The Lord, the God of heaven, has given me all the kingdoms of the earth and has appointed me to build Him a house at Jerusalem in Judah."* (HCSB)

We might be caused to wonder why Cyrus did not personally take charge of the city and whether there is a contradiction in Daniel 5:31, where we find that *"Darius the Median took the kingdom, being about threescore and two years old"* (KJV). There is no difficulty here, since

> *Prideaux tells us that Darius was the uncle of Cyrus and "Cyrus allowed him the title of all his conquests as long as he lived." After Darius died, however, Cyrus became the sole leader of the kingdom* (Daniel 6:28).[126]

---

[124] Woodrow, *Great Prophecies*, 88–89, 94.
[125] Ibid., 93–94.
[126] Ibid., 92.

This is further corroborated by the Jewish historian Josephus:

> ...and this is the end of the posterity of King Nebuchadnezzar, as history informs us; but when Babylon was taken by Darius, and when he, with his kinsmen Cyrus, had put an end to the dominion of the Babylonians, he was sixty-two years old.[127]

GALLIO WHO?

Moving into the New Testament, we find that here, too, the spade of the archaeologist is a friend to Bible truth. In Acts 18:12–17, we find reference made to Gallio, the Roman proconsul, a man whose existence was denied by critics for years. They asserted that he never was a ruler in Corinth, as reported in the Scriptures. The critics are now evoking a deafening silence as they have been proven wrong in their assertions. The record of this man has been uncovered deep in the soil of ancient Corinth, with his name found written on a two-thousand-year-old inscription, thus confirming the biblical account. Indeed, you can trust your Bible!

This notation comes from the Apologetics Study Bible:

> The date of Gallio's time as proconsul of Achaia (Corinth was its capital) is a firm one in NT chronology. An inscription dated to AD 52 refers to him when he was no longer proconsul. Thus, Gallio was installed as proconsul in early AD 51 and Paul appeared before him later that year. Gallio noted nothing that defied Rome's tolerant religious laws.[128]

PETER AND PAUL AT ODDS?

The latter part of the nineteenth century saw the rise of higher criticism, which we will comment on later in more detail. The critics of that time were convinced that the apostle Peter took a far different view on Christianity than did the apostle Paul, thereby creating a rift between them in the early stages of the New Testament Church. The widely accepted theory was that the book of Acts was a well-concocted second-century fabrication designed to cover up the rift between the two men. The Acts of the Apostles was not treated as authentic history and Luke's authorship was dismissed as forgery.

---

[127] William Whiston, trans., *The Works of Josephus* (Peabody, MA: Hendrickson, 1987), 226.
[128] *Apologetics Study Bible*, 1656.

One of the critics was the brilliant chemist and Noble Prize winner Sir William Ramsey, who, keeping an open mind, determined to test this theory against the evidence yielded by archaeological research. For years, he studied the discoveries of archaeological inquiry in the Mediterranean and studied ancient life in Eastern Europe and Asia Minor. Sifting through all the evidence, he became convinced that the book of Acts was written by Luke in the first century. He further found that the events given in Acts are historically accurate and that Peter and Paul worked in concert with each other, discounting their alleged conflict as pure fabrication.[129]

---

[129] Criswell, *Why I Preach*, 56.

CHAPTER EIGHT

Transformed

The dramatic change in the lives of millions of human beings throughout the two thousand years of church history is further proof of the persuasive power that is latent in the words of Scripture. Many are the individuals who have found themselves captivated by the power of God's Word even as they struggled in vain to escape from the Holy Spirit's work of conviction exercised through the words of Scripture. A reading of Hebrews 11 reminds us that God's Word was also at work in the lives of Old Testament individuals, including Enoch, Abraham, and Moses, whose testimonies reach down through the centuries to encourage and inspire believers to the present day.

Following is a list of just a few believers whose testimonies bear witness to the powerful influence of God's Word in their lives.

THE ETHIOPIAN EUNUCH

The unfolding events that transpire in Acts 8 are directly related to the terrible persecution then raging against the early church. Feeding off the enthusiasm of powerful leaders, including the fanatically Jewish Saul of Tarsus, opponents of Christianity had killed Stephen, forcing many others to flee to other regions. One of those persons was Philip, who had gone to the city of Samaria to preach the gospel. This city was the former capital of the northern kingdom of Israel, which had been conquered by the Assyrians in the latter part of the eighth century B.C. We are reminded that both Stephen and Philip were two of the seven chosen men in Acts 6:1–5.

The people of Samaria had only the writings of Moses (the first five books of the Old Testament), but prompted by the preaching of Philip, they responded in mass numbers to the gospel message. This great religious awakening followed Philip as he ministered in numerous Samaritan villages on his way back to Jerusalem. Then, he was suddenly advised by an angel to change course and travel the road to Gaza (Acts 8:25–26). On that road, he encountered a high official from the royal household of Ethiopia intently reading from the book of Isaiah as he travelled home from Jerusalem. As the men engaged in conversation, the eunuch admitted to Philip that he was puzzled by what he was reading and needed someone to help him understand the writing before him.

Inviting Philip to join him in his carriage, the Ethiopian soon embraced the truth of the gospel and was baptized by the evangelist. The Scriptures tell us what happened next:

> *And when they were come up out of the water, the Spirit of the Lord caught away Philip, that the eunuch saw him no more: and he went on his way rejoicing.* (Acts 8:39, KJV)

Many church historians believe that this East African official became the driving force behind the spread of the gospel in Ethiopia and further into the inner regions of Africa. Thomas Walker remarks,

> Tradition represents him as the evangelist of Ethiopia, and the Abyssians regard him, though without sufficient reason, as the founder of their church.[130]

THE APOSTLE PAUL

Considered by some students of history to be the greatest influence on European civilization over the last two thousand years, Paul's astounding conversion is recounted for us in Acts 9 and repeated as his testimony in Acts 22 and 26. Formerly a leading persecutor of the early church and one of the most highly educated Jewish Pharisees of his time, his conversion and subsequent ministry angered the Jews but was widely received by the Gentiles, who became his focus

---

[130] Thomas Walker, *The Acts of the Apostles* (Chicago, IL: Moody Press, 1965), 202.

for gospel preaching (Acts 13:46). According to some reports, Paul's physical appearance may have offended some. From Herbert Lochyer's writings, we have this description of the Apostle Paul:

> Paul's bodily size and appearance may have been against him, judging from a second century apocryphal description of him. "He was a man little of stature, partly bald, with crooked legs, of vigorous physique, with eyes set close together and nose somewhat hooked." What he was in his appearance mattered little. Paul lived only to win others to Christ and to make Him known.[131]

In spite of this, Paul's ministry had a very positive impact on the early church. In 2 Corinthians 11, Paul catalogues for us the many times he faced physical and emotional suffering due to his passionate commitment to gospel ministry. Tradition tells us that Paul's life ended in Rome, where he was beheaded by a Roman executioner. No less than thirteen New Testament books came from his hand, and many believe he authored the book of Hebrews, bringing the number to fourteen. The book of Romans is, undoubtedly, the masterpiece of all his writings.

AURELIUS AUGUSTINE (354–430)

Augustine's writings were standard fare for clergy for well over a thousand years and his influence was evident throughout the Protestant Reformation. He was born at Jagaste, in Numidia, a province of North Africa, in 345 A.D. He gave his life to unbridled pleasure in his early years and moved a woman into his home whom he never married. While pursuing studies in Carthage, he became father to a son, Adeodatus, in 372. He was intellectually brilliant and was prayed for regularly by his Christian mother, Monica, whose prayers were answered when her son was converted. The change in his life was immediate, and shortly afterward his live-in companion was put out of his home.

Coming to faith in 387, Augustine was destined for a long and active life of ministry. He became the Bishop of Hippo in North Africa and developed into a prolific writer. His writings included his *Confessions*, which describes his life and state of mind prior to his conversion, as well as *The City of God*, in which he speaks prophetically of a Christian society destined to develop and grow in influence just as the mighty Roman Empire was falling apart. By the time of his

---

[131] Herbert Lochyer, *All the Men of the Bible* (Grand Rapids, MI: Zondervan, 1958), 270.

death in 430, he had established himself as one of the greatest theological minds in the history of the church.

> The central tenets of his creed were the corruption of human nature through the fall of Man, the consequent slavery of the human will, predestination and the perseverance of the Saints.[132]

By the time of Augustine's death, the gates of Hippo in North Africa were being breached by the Vandals, who had already become the masters of Africa's northern coast.

> And yet, his work was not forgotten among the ruins of a crumbling civilization. On the contrary, through his writings, he became the teacher of the new age. Throughout the Middle Ages, no theologian was quoted more often than he was, and he thus became one of the great doctors of the Roman Catholic Church. But he was also the favorite theologian of the great Protestant reformers of the sixteenth century. Thus Augustine, variously interpreted, has become the most influential theologian in the entire Western church both Protestant and Catholic.[133]

MARTIN LUTHER (1483–1546)

Martin Luther has been called by some the "apostle of the sixteenth century" and the "father of the Reformation." Born the son of a miner in 1483, he received his arts degree from the University of Erfurt in Germany in 1502. Much to the chagrin of his parents, he shortly afterward entered a monastery in an effort to find a meaningful relationship with God. For years he remained in ongoing turmoil within his own soul, but through the reading of the Scriptures, especially the books of Psalms and Romans, he came to saving faith in the Lord Jesus Christ, thereupon entering a lifetime of conflict with the Roman Catholic Church. He married a nun, raised six children, and became the voice of Protestants everywhere.[134]

On October 31, 1517, Luther posted his ninety-five theses, voicing his opposition to the selling of indulgences by the representatives of the Catholic

[132] Una McGovern, ed., *Chambers Biographical Dictionary* (Edinburgh, UK: Chambers Harrap Publishers, 2005), 81.

[133] Justo L. González, *The Story of Christianity, Volume 1: The Early Church to the Dawn of the Reformation* (Peabody, MA: Prince Press, 2004), 216–217.

[134] Justo L. González, *The Story of Christianity, Volume 2: The Reformation to the Present Day* (Peabody, MA: Prince Press, 2004), 15–16.

Church.[135] His public protest shook the church of Rome to its foundations and changed the course of church history forever. He refused to recant and on many occasions required the protection of the political authorities, who were weary of Roman Catholic corruption and excesses.[136]

Luther taught and preached the Scriptures at every opportunity. In 1522, he translated the New Testament into German, and in 1534 he gave the German people the Old Testament in their own language. He also wrote a number of hymns, including "A Mighty Fortress Is Our God." The printers of Martin Luther's day were kept busy by the great reformer, with some estimates suggesting he published writings on average every three weeks. In 1529, he published his *Small Catechism*, which presented the truths of Scripture in a refreshing and simple manner as a tool of instruction for the many people in rural churches who were woefully uninformed about the most basic teachings of the Bible.[137]

Some of the more refined elements of today's church would find difficulty with some of Martin Luther's mannerisms. His language was often coarse, his temperament one of great impatience, and he often drank beer with his meals. Luther and his followers also retained infant baptism and opposed the mode of immersion, which was practised by the early church. To his credit, he had great affection for his wife and children, and they admired him for his strength of character and evident love for the cause of Christ. In a book entitled *Invitation to the Classics*, where the writings of Martin Luther are given high marks for theological depth and intellectual integrity, the following tribute is given to the man who placed conscience above tradition:

> In short, Luther was not impeccable. But he was a man gripped by a mighty vision of God. It was this vision of God that shook him to the depths of his own being, broke through the religious conventions of his day, and compelled nearly the whole world to pay attention.[138]

John DeSalvo notes that Martin Luther's Bible, which was published in 1534, "gained instant popularity largely because of accessibility of its language...

---

[135] Perry F. Rockwood, *Romanism and the Bible with Luther's 95 Thesis* (Halifax, NS: The People's Gospel Hour), 4–10.

[136] González, *Story of Christianity, Volume 2*, 24–26.

[137] Roland H. Bainton, *Here I Stand: A Life of Martin Luther* (New York, NY: Mentor Books, The New American Library, 1950), 255, 263, 270–271.

[138] Louise Cowan and Os Guinness, eds., *Invitation to the Classics* (Grand Rapids, MI: Baker Books, 1998), 122.

[and it] remains in print to this day."[139] In terms of durability, his Bible must be considered a classic work. He singlehandedly gave the German people a Bible in their mother tongue nearly eighty years before the King James translators gave their landmark version to the English people.

One author has pointed out that, though Martin Luther is known by many labels—including reformer, scholar, teacher, husband, father, composer, and prayer warrior—many forget that he was also a prolific preacher.

> From the beginning of his ministry in 1512 to his death in 1546 he preached over four thousand sermons. Even in years when his health was bad, Luther would often preach nearly two hundred times. Generally, he averaged three sermons per week throughout his adult life, but often preached four or more. Luther was, to state it mildly, a homiletical force.[140]

As with all other aspects of his ministry, Luther worked hard at making himself intelligible to his listeners. He said that a preacher who was sincere about his ministry

> must consider the young people, the servants and the maids in the church, those who lack education. He must accommodate himself to them as a nursing mother does to her infant… [and] preachers should be… simple in their sermons.[141]

Using his own children for illustrative purposes, Luther shows his skill as a marvellous communicator, "adapting language to the audience's level of understanding… [communicating] in such a way that even the youngest parishioner can hear and understand."[142] As Luther taught his students, keeping the sermon clear and crisp, so that even the youngest could understand it, was of paramount importance. Even with the inevitable frustrations, no effort was to be spared in reaching out to every age level.

> I will not consider Drs. Pomeranus, Jonas and Phillip while I am preaching; for they know what I am presenting better than I do. Nor do

---

[139] John DeSalvo, *Dead Sea Scrolls* (Toronto, ON: Indigo Books & Music, 2008), 56.
[140] Keith Willhite and Scott M. Gibson, eds., *The Big Idea of Biblical Preaching* (Grand Rapids, MI: Baker Books, 1998), 31.
[141] Ibid., 33.
[142] Ibid., 32.

I preach to them, but to my little Hans and Elizabeth: these I consider. He must be a harebrained gardener who wants to consider only one flower in a large garden and neglects all the others. Therefore, see to it that you preach plainly and simply and have regard for the unlearned people and do not address only one or the other.[143]

Luther believed that preaching should be both relevant and biblical.

The closing years of Martin Luther's life were filled with activity, as they always had been. He had no intention of watching the grass grow. He could look back on a life filled with God's evident blessing. In 1525, he had married the twenty-six-year-old Katherine von Bora. She was one of nine nuns who had left (some would say escaped) life in a convent.[144] In the face of opposition to the marriage, Katherine proved to be an ideal wife for the forty-two-year-old Luther. They were blessed with three sons (Hans, Martin, and Paul) and three daughters (Magdalena, Elizabeth, and Margaretha), with the last dying at fourteen, bringing great sorrow to the Luther home. Four orphaned children were also taken into the family circle.[145]

Among the accomplishments of the great German reformer, of which there are many, perhaps the most enduring and influential was his translation of the Bible. He continued to tweak it and improve it to the end of his life. Coming on the scene sixteen years before the 1560 Geneva Bible, it is still being used by the German people. The English owe a debt of gratitude to this German translator. His preface found its way into William Tyndale's New Testament. *The Book of Common Prayer* drew heavily on his liturgical reforms.

The Reformation in Germany cut a pathway for his English counterparts. Unlike the English, Luther did not have to deal with an unruly and unreasonable Henry VIII or a mean-spirited Queen Mary, who determined to keep the fields of Smithfield well lit with a seemingly endless supply of human torches. Luther had won the respect of countless politicians who admired his sense of passion and vision for his great cause.

When the year 1546 dawned upon the human race, Martin Luther's days were coming to a close. He had suffered much through the years with a litany of medical problems, including gout, hemorrhoids, and dizziness, with the added burden of a lifelong battle with unrelenting depression. His "rib," as he affectionately called Katie, patiently looked after the "Doctor," the appellation she always employed when addressing her famous husband.

---

[143] Ibid.
[144] McGovern, *Chambers Biographical Dictionary*, 958.
[145] Bainton, *Here I Stand*, 224–225, 229, 237.

His last act of human kindness was to settle a dispute between the counts of Mansfeld, who so esteemed the German reformer that they insisted he come and be their mediator. With this matter brought to a successful conclusion, Luther's earthly frame was simply worn out. His labours ended with his passing at Eisleben and subsequent burial at Wittenburg.[146]

POCAHONTAS (1595–1617): CONVERSION OF A PRINCESS

Located twenty-four kilometres inland from Chesapeake Bay, the site of the first successful British settlement in America is now a deserted town. Founded in 1607, this piece of American history was the focus of an archaeological dig from 1934–1956, which had yielded enough evidence to successfully outline the fort which used to stand on the spot. It was to this town that the daughter of Chief Powhatan was taken by the English as a captive in 1612. We know her as Pocahontas (meaning "playful one"), which was the nickname given her by her father (known as Matoaka, or Amonute). She was born in 1595 to one of the more than one hundred wives of her father. She is said to have saved the life of one John Smith, but their friendship did not lead to marriage. She converted to Christianity as a teenager, taking the name Rebecca on the occasion of her baptism. On April 5, 1614, she married a well-to-do widower ten years her senior whose name was John Rolfe. Their only child, Thomas, was born on January 30, 1615. Their marriage was the first recorded of that between an Englishman and a Native American woman.

The family travelled to England together, where this good-natured and attractive woman was introduced to King James I of England and his wife, Anne of Denmark. The new settlement from which they had departed in Virginia (named after the Virgin Queen, Elizabeth) was named Jamestown. In 2007, Jamestown, named for the British king, celebrated four hundred years since its settlement, and one of the visitors on this historic occasion was Queen Elizabeth II, a direct descendant of James I. In fact, she is his great-great-great-great-great-great-great-great-great-great-great-granddaughter.

The queen returned to the place where Pocahontas and John Rolfe had met four hundred years earlier. Elizabeth II returned home safely following her visit, but such was not the good fortune of the Native American princess four centuries earlier. Pocahontas died of smallpox on her return journey in 1617, just off the coast of England.[147] Some notable descendants of Pocahontas include first ladies Edith Wilson and Nancy Reagan, actor Glenn Strange,

[146] Ibid, 300–302, 227–229.
[147] McGovern, "Pocahontas," *Chambers Biographic Dictionary*, 1215.

and astronomer and mathematician Percival Lowell, who helped discover the planet Pluto.

Towns named after Pocahontas can be found in the states of Virginia, Iowa, Arkansas, Illinois, and Mississippi, as well as the province of Alberta in Canada.[148]

WILLIAM CAREY (1761–1834)

The man who has become known as the father of modern missions was born into a poor family in Northampshire, England in 1761. William Carey recalled how the Scriptures were read regularly in his home and at the Anglican Church where his family worshipped. He especially recalled the reading of the Psalms during the worship services of his home church but knew very little of experiential religion until his early teens. He had apprenticed as a shoemaker in his mid-teens at a place seven miles from his home. There he met a fellow apprentice by the name of John Warr, a Congregationalist and committed Christian whose witness was used of God to bring Carey to a saving knowledge of the Lord Jesus Christ. At first Carey was resistant, but at some point in 1779 he embraced the claims of Christ on his life.

Several years after his conversion, this young Englishman became convinced from the Scriptures that infant baptism was an unscriptural practice, thus alienating himself from both Anglicans and Congregationalists. He was baptized on October 5, 1785, by John Ryland Jr., whose father was the pastor of College Lane Baptist Church in North Hampton. Following his baptism in the River Nene, Carey determined to learn more about the nations beyond the shores of England, many of whom had never heard a word of the gospel.[149]

After holding several pastorates in England, Carey left for India in 1793, where he served in the work of evangelism for over forty years. By the time of his passing in 1834, many thousands had come to Christ and his bold and ambitious approach to missions had encouraged many others to follow his example.[150]

He, along with John Ryland Jr. (his baptizer), Andrew Fuller, and John Sutcliff, had formed the Baptist Missionary Society before he left the shores of England. This pioneer society, which became Carey's primary means of support, set the pace for other missionary enterprises to come. It is noteworthy that Carey's conviction to take the gospel to India came straight from the words of

[148] Wikipedia, "Pocahontas." Date of access: November 19, 2015 (https://en.wikipedia.org/wiki/Pocahontas).
[149] H. Leon McBeth, *The Baptist Heritage* (Nashville, TN: Broadman Press, 1987), 143.
[150] Lewis A. Drummond, *The Canvas Cathedral* (Nashville, TN: Thomas Nelson Publishers, 2003), 443–445.

Scripture. His study of Matthew 28:18–20 convinced him that this command was to be obeyed by every Christian until the return of the Lord.[151] Carey's accomplishments included the founding of the Serampur Mission in India (1799) as well as a professorship at Fort William College in Calcutta (1801–1830).[152]

HENRY ALLINE (1748–1784)

Born in Newport, Rhode Island in 1748, Henry Alline moved with his parents to Falmouth, Nova Scotia in 1760. He was raised in a Christian home where he early on became acquainted with the Scriptures, but he was twenty-seven years old before he began to seriously consider his relationship to the Lord. His conversion came after an agonizing and profound struggle, culminating in an emotional and life-changing experience that became the turning point and central event of his life. Little did anyone suspect that he would become Nova Scotia's most gifted preacher and most prolific hymn-writer. Sadly, most Christians today have never heard of the one who would become known as the "apostle to Nova Scotia."

His ministry of less than ten years saw him preach numerous times throughout Nova Scotia and present-day New Brunswick. His travels are documented in his journal, which was published in 1806, but the original copy has been lost to us for over a hundred years. His most effective ministry seems to have been in the Yarmouth area of Nova Scotia and New Brunswick, especially in Hartland and surrounding area. He is mentioned numerous times in the diaries of Simeon Perkins of Liverpool.[153]

Though Alline was thoroughly evangelical, his doctrinal views have been a continuing source of confusion and controversy. He lacked formal education and was unable, due to some unfortunate circumstances, to pursue ministerial training in the United States. He wrote over five hundred hymns, and records tell us that he was an excellent singer. Though not a Baptist, he nonetheless became the catalyst for a sweeping revival in the Maritimes that, shortly following his early death at the age of thirty-six, would lay the groundwork for the strong Baptist presence that is still with us today. The Convention of Atlantic Baptist Churches, which consists of over five hundred churches in the Maritimes and Newfoundland, was brought about as a direct result of the religious movement spawned by the influence of Alline's ministry.

---

[151] González, *Story of Christianity, Volume 2*, 306–307, 309, 311, 321.

[152] McGovern, "William Carey," *Chambers Biographical Dictionary*, 273.

[153] James Beverley and Barry Moody, eds., *The Journal of Henry Alline* (Hantsport, NS: Lancelot Press, 1982), 10, 20, 22–23.

A vivid description of the Falmouth preacher has been left to us in the writings of Mrs. Fox, the daughter of one of Alline's early converts. From her perspective in 1856, it seems that Alline was a most persuasive and riveting speaker. In her ninety-third year, she could still recall a sermon that was preached by Alline in 1780, a full seventy-six years earlier. She remembered some of his words and she knew the text (John 12:35) from which he had drawn his sermon. She also shared that Alline had little time for idle conversation but would talk incessantly about spiritual matters.[154]

Central to Alline's ministry and the spiritual awakening that it brought to Nova Scotia was the Bible. This was well attested to in 1948, when Maurice Armstrong published his book, *The Great Awakening in Nova Scotia, 1776–1809*. The book examined this crucial time in the spiritual life of Nova Scotia against the backdrop of the American Revolution and the powerful preaching and presence of Henry Alline.

The following statement is from James Beverley and Barry Moody, who have given us an edited version of Alline's journal:

> Stress on Alline as a mystic or enthusiast has taken attention from the large role that Scripture has in the development and shape of Alline and his theology. He refers to the Bible as the "infallible and unerring Word" of God. Biblical quotations and allusions abound in his two theology books, in his three published sermons, and also serve as the background for his hymnology. Similarly, the journal contains about two hundred quotations from the Bible or clear allusions to Biblical events or phrases. In the journal alone he utilizes material from sixteen Old Testament books and sixteen New Testament books.[155]

The early part of 1783 witnessed the rapid deterioration of Alline's health. He was suffering from tuberculosis and facing near death when he returned to his roots in New England. He did not go empty-handed. Besides copies of his published material, he took his journal in shorthand and five hundred of his hymns in manuscript form. He reached northern Maine in September and on February 2, 1784, he died in New Hampshire.[156]

In 1975, one of Alline's sermons (highly edited) was published in Billy Graham's *Decision* magazine. There is something that catches our attention here.

[154] George Rawlyk, ed., *The Sermons of Henry Alline* (Hantsport, NS: Lancelot Press, 1982), 18.
[155] Beverley and Moody, *Journal of Henry Alline*, 22.
[156] Rawlyk, *Sermons of Henry Alline*, 18.

Decision's editor prefaced the sermon with the words, "Canadians will never forget the preacher who brought the Great Awakening to Nova Scotia";[157] but the truth is that we have long ago forgotten Henry Alline, who has probably had greater impact in the United States than in Canada. This is a vivid illustration of the elements of contradiction that seemed to follow the Falmouth, Nova Scotia preacher around most of his life. While preaching a strong free will Arminian position, Alline yet believed in the perseverance of the saints.

Even in his passing there was a strange dichotomy at work. Sickness prevented Alline from continuing his diary past November 18, 1783. His final days were spent among a group of ministers who were strongly Calvinistic,[158] a theological persuasion that Alline hated and had preached against for years.[159] The man who cared for the ailing evangelist from Nova Scotia in his closing days on earth was the deeply Calvinistic but kind-hearted Rev. David McClure, whose closest associates were also committed Calvinists. These godly pastors from in and around North Hampton, New Hampshire, became the officiants at Alline's funeral service as well as his pallbearers. Alline was laid to rest at a local cemetery near the grave of Rev. Mr. Gookin, former pastor of McClure's church.

The closing lines of David McClure's letter to Alline's parents in Falmouth tells something of the spirit and testimony of their son:

> As I doubt not, Sir, from your worthy son's frequent mention of you, that you and his honoured mother have long walked with God, that it might afford you unspeakable satisfaction, that you have been blessed with such a son, and have the triumphant hope of speedily meeting him, no more to part, in the bright region of eternal day.[160]

The son of William and Rebecca Alline left behind a horse and sleigh, some clothing, twelve dollars, and a vibrant testimony. His thoughts on Bible study are worth noting:

> I believe that many Men would increase much in spiritual Wealth, if they would give themselves the Trouble of digging for it; but they too often neglect to do it, because they imagine, that their good old Fathers

---

[157] Ibid., 21.

[158] The doctrines of John Calvin put a heavy accent on predestination and irresistible grace.

[159] So strong were his Arminian sentiments that the Reverend Jonathan Scott, Calvinist pastor at the Congregational Church in Yarmouth, was forced to leave his dwindling congregation and return to the United States.

[160] Beverley and Moody, *Journal of Henry Alline*, 223.

have dug deep enough. But as the Word of God is yet an inexhaustible Fund, make that your chief Study…[161]

CHARLES SPURGEON (1834–1892)

As a young boy, this future pastor struggled for more than five years with fear and distress about his spiritual state. He was raised in a Christian home and had attended numerous places of worship but was convinced he had yet to hear a clear presentation of the gospel. In a blinding snowstorm on his way to a familiar place of worship one Sunday morning, he found it impossible to continue any farther, so he turned down a side street where he found a little Primitive Methodist chapel. From Spurgeon's personal account, about fifteen people came to this service and the minister did not show up.

A man from the congregation, obviously poor and unlearned, got up from the gathering and made his way to the pulpit, where he proceeded to give a brief message from Isaiah 45:22. Using the word *look* for emphasis, he gave a very simple gospel message that spoke to the heart of Spurgeon, resulting in his immediate conversion. That morning, a boy in his early teens left the chapel fully transformed and rejoicing in his salvation experience. After academic training at Maidstone Agricultural College, he became a tutor for several years.[162]

Charles Spurgeon began preaching at sixteen years of age, and in his nineteenth year he became the pastor of New Park Street Chapel in Southwark, London. In 1861, his ministry was transferred to the newly consecrated Baptist Tabernacle on Kensington Road, where he remained until his death in 1892. He was never ordained, had no ministerial training, and declined a number of honorary degrees that were offered to him. Incredibly, at the age of twenty he began to publish a sermon every week. He also authored a number of works, ranging from devotional to expository to homiletical to literary.[163]

Spurgeon read voraciously, studying not only the Bible, but history, science, astronomy, and literature. His huge library contained thousands of volumes, and he was familiar with every book. Some observers are convinced that Spurgeon had no organized filing system for his many books, but he knew his authors well and his collection was organized accordingly. He was able to find any book on the shelf as needed with a moment's notice.[164]

---

[161] Ibid., 234.

[162] Dr. Michael Haykin, *The Life and Legacy of Charles Haddon Spurgeon (1834–1892)* (Canadian Publications Mail Product Sales, Spurgeon Ministries), 3–4.

[163] Iain H. Murray, *The Forgotten Spurgeon* (London, UK: The Banner of Truth Trust, 1966), 31–32.

[164] Ibid., 41.

Over five thousand people attended each of Spurgeon's two Sunday services, and during many of those services over seven hundred of his men met in the basement for prayer.[165] The New Park Street Baptist Church of London welcomed their nineteen-year-old pastor with eighty people on his first Sunday. The building could hold 1,500 people, but the congregation was struggling during this dry spell in their ministry. All of this would change in dramatic fashion. Within that first year, over two thousand people crowded their way into the services, making expansion of the building a necessity. They were strangely drawn and sat spellbound as their young preacher delivered the Word of God in a way to which they were not accustomed.[166]

In 1859–1861, the Metropolitan Tabernacle was erected with a seating capacity for six thousand. Spurgeon remained there until his passing in 1892. The building later burned down.[167]

He also opened a pastor's college in 1856 for the express purpose of training young pastors. Spurgeon received no pay for his lectures and teaching ministry here. He encouraged God's people to support the college with their prayers and finances so that those who were gifted for ministry would not be hindered from entering the college due to insufficient funds. He further emphasized that the purpose of the college was to train preachers, not scholars. Over the years, Spurgeon has become known as the "prince of preachers," an appellation he richly deserved.

The college that Spurgeon founded is now known as Spurgeon's Theological College. As Drummond notes,

> It serves to this day and ministers as the largest Baptist theological school in Britain. Many notables have come through that institution and taken their ranks as missionaries, evangelists, professors, and pastors around the world.[168]

Spurgeon established an orphanage in 1869, which grew to house five hundred disadvantaged children. He loved the children and often visited with them, to their great delight. He had requested he be buried on the orphanage grounds, but his wish was not granted.[169]

[165] Jesse Lyman Hurlbut, ed., *Sunday Half Hours with Great Preachers* (Chicago, IL: W.E. Scull, 1907), 521.

[166] Drummond, *The Canvas Cathedral*, 479.

[167] McGovern, "Charles Haddon Spurgeon," *Chambers Biographical Dictionary*, 1426.

[168] Drummond, *The Canvas Cathedral*, 480.

[169] Haykin, *Life and Legacy*, 6–7.

A book fund was established by Spurgeon and his wife, Susannah, who became the director of this charitable agency for Christian workers. Books were supplied freely to workers who lacked the funds to purchase them. A monthly magazine entitled *The Sword and the Trowel* began publication in 1865.[170]

The reading habits of Charles Spurgeon were nothing short of astounding. He averaged six books every week, and his reading reflected his theological persuasion, especially in the matter of the salvation experience. He was unabashedly Calvinistic, believing that all who came to Christ did so only by the electing grace of God. This was also taught by the Puritans, whose writings were strongly represented in Spurgeon's massive library.

> Spurgeon's opinion of the Puritans with whom he was first acquainted in his childhood, remained with him all his days. He said in 1872, "We assert this day that, when we take down a volume of Puritanical theology we find in a solitary page more thinking and more learning, more Scripture, more real teaching, than in whole folios of the effusions of modern thought. The modern men would be rich if they possessed even the crumbs that fall from the table of the Puritans."[171]

Soul-winning was front and centre in all of Spurgeon's ministry, which positioned him for sharp criticism from both hyper-Calvinists and Arminians. The hyper-Calvinists felt he was too free with the public invitation, while the Arminians objected to his strong emphasis on sovereignty, which to them presented an insuperable barrier to the seeking sinner.

Iain H. Murray says,

> The point at which he diverged from both Hyper-Calvinism and Arminianism is that he refused to rationalize *how* men can be commanded to do what is not in their power. Arminians say that sinners are commanded, therefore they must be able; Hyper-Calvinists say they are not able, therefore they cannot be commanded. But Scripture and Calvinism sets forth *both* man's inability and his duty, and both truths are a necessary part of evangelism—the former reveals the sinner's need of a help which only God can give, and the latter, which is expressed in the exhortations, promises and invitations of Scripture, shows him the

---

[170] Ibid., 7.
[171] Murray, *Forgotten Spurgeon*, 42.

place in which his peace and safety lies, namely the Person of the Son of God.[172]

Spurgeon's answer to what appears to some to be a theological conundrum is as follows:

> The same difficulty is raised when it is asked, How can men be responsible when they perish in sin if grace alone can prevent such an end? Someone says, "But I do not understand this doctrine." Perhaps not, but remember that, while we are bound to tell you the truth, we are not bound to give you the power to understand it; and besides, this is not a subject for understanding, it is a matter for believing because it is revealed in the Word of God. It is one of the axioms of theology that, if man is saved, God must have all the glory of it.[173]

The work and influence of Charles Spurgeon reached far and beyond his pulpit ministry.

> Not since the days of the Apostle Paul were so many people turned to the Lord. But what else followed? These blessings were added: Homes for widows, orphanages for destitute children, colportage societies that bring the Word of God to those who do not possess it, and missionaries to preach the message of salvation beyond the seas. From that one man's preaching of the Bible, marvelous influences flowed out over the world. A man was found frozen to death in the Alps. He had one of Spurgeon's sermons in his hand. When David Livingstone died, he had one of Spurgeon's sermons in the top of his hat. The influence of the preaching of the Bible by Spurgeon in the Metropolitan Tabernacle in London literally moved the whole world Godward.[174]

The latter part of the eighteenth century saw the incursion of liberal theology into the Baptist churches of England. So incensed was Spurgeon with this betrayal of biblical principles that he led his church out of the Baptist Union. Known as the Down-Grade Controversy, this emotional and protracted struggle consumed the last five years of the London preacher's life. He developed kidney disease, and

[172] Ibid., 105–106.
[173] Ibid., 105.
[174] Criswell, *Why I Preach*, 17.

before leaving for France on October 26, 1891, he stated to his friends, "The fight is killing me." He had hoped to get some respite, along with relief of his painful condition at Mentone, to where he had often repaired, but such was not to be. On February 1, 1892, the public received news that the beloved pastor of the Metropolitan Tabernacle had slipped away the day before, a Sunday. There is no doubt in the minds of those who have studied Spurgeon's remarkable life that the Down-Grade Controversy brought about his premature passing. His death brought to a close a thirty-eight-year ministry that had commenced in the spring of 1854. His last sermon was delivered June 7, 1891.[175]

The influence of Charles Spurgeon is felt to the present time. This can be no better seen than in the voluminous writings he left behind: "To the present day, there remain more books in print written by Spurgeon than by any other English author of any literary genre."[176] There are those who may cavil over his uncompromising conviction as to the place of God's sovereignty in God's redemptive plan, but his very positive contribution to the cause of righteousness cannot be denied. His commitment to ministry at the Metropolitan Tabernacle is testimony to his great love for Christ and His church. It was from his chosen venue of local church ministry at Park Street that he was enabled to plant "more than two hundred new congregations in Great Britain."[177]

The passing of Charles Spurgeon stirred the soul of Great Britain as few people have before or since. His desire had been for a simple service, with only "C.H.S." inscribed on his tombstone, but his church and the nation would have none of it.

> After the return of his body to England it "lay in state" at the Tabernacle, with as many as 50,000 mourners coming to pay their last respects. On the actual day of the funeral, thousands lined the streets along which the funeral procession passed, with shops, and even pubs, closing their doors for the day. His body was laid to rest in an ornate tomb; on top of the coffin in which it was placed was a Bible open at the very text instrumental in his conversion so many years before. "Look unto me, and be ye saved, all the ends of the earth: for I am God, and there is none else" (Isaiah 45:22).[178]

---

[175] Murray, *Forgotten Spurgeon*, 159–161, 168–171.
[176] Drummond, *The Canvas Cathedral*, 482.
[177] Ibid.
[178] Haykin, *Life and Legacy*, 12.

BILLY SUNDAY (1862–1935)

We will probably never see Billy Sunday's like again, and if accounts handed down to us are accurate, we can only conclude that this former major league baseball player was one of the most sensational evangelists the church has ever unleashed on an unsuspecting world. His style would be an embarrassment to the church in this politically correct postmodern era, but the results speak for themselves. Over a million souls came to Christ through his ministry, with countless lives and homes transformed for the cause of righteousness. Assisted by a well-organized team of workers, including choir leader Homer A. Rodeheaver, he conducted over three hundred revival meetings, with a total attendance estimated in excess of one hundred million.[179] Such was his penetrating influence that many towns where Sunday preached saw their movie houses, brothels, and bars shut down for want of business.[180]

Scenes and people from the Bible came alive as Sunday acted out Bible events in a way that captured the rapt attention of the congregation. He commandeered the entire platform, never standing still. He was known to stand on the pulpit, and sometimes furniture, including the pulpit, would be broken by some well-landed blows from the energetic preacher. Much of the organization—including great music, follow-up, cottage prayer meetings, and energized leadership—that is seen today in evangelistic services was passed down to us from Billy Sunday and others long before our present-day crusades and festivals.[181]

Where did all of this begin for William Ashley Sunday? On a Sunday afternoon in Chicago, with an inebriated Sunday sitting on the curb listening to a lively service conducted by the Pacific Garden Mission. Stirred by what he heard, he responded to the invitation and gave his heart to Christ. By the age of thirty-four, he was in full-time evangelism, with some of his tabernacles filled to capacity with over twenty thousand people.[182] He died in 1935 at the age of seventy-two.

Billy Sunday's ministry was characterized by belief in the truth of the Bible and the faithful preaching of God's plan of salvation to all who would listen. In a 1933 meeting, he stated his convictions clearly, as he had done hundreds of times before:

---

[179] "William Ashley Sunday," *Encyclopaedia Britannica, Inc., Volume 21* (Toronto, ON: William Benton, 1961), 566.

[180] Elijah P. Brown, *The Real Billy Sunday* (Chattanooga, TN: Global Publishers, 1914), 209–210.

[181] Ibid., 99, 106–108, 140, 144–152.

[182] Lee Thomas, *The Billy Sunday Story* (Murfreesboro, TN: Sword of the Lord Publishers, 2005), 225–227.

I believe in the absolute Deity of Jesus, His virgin birth, His atoning death, His resurrection from the dead, His future coming in glory, and the hopeless, helpless state of men aside from the redeeming work of Christ.[183]

His preaching was practical and pointed; he said it with pithy notations like this one: "There are men in Hell because they wasted too much time trying to find out where Cain got his wife."[184]

CHARLOTTE ELLIOTT (1789–1871)

Born in 1789, this little known lady was an invalid for the last fifty of her eighty-two years. Shortly after her body became incapacitated, Charlotte received a visit from a Dr. Milan, who became concerned about her soul's salvation. Feeling she would not be accepted by Christ as she was, she rejected his appeal to give her heart to Christ. She later relented and accepted the good doctor's encouragement to come to Christ.

A full twelve years later, we find a depressed and physically challenged woman upset that she was unable to help the other ladies with a bazaar which had been proposed for the next day. Charlotte lay awake most of the night, but the next morning she recalled the words of Dr. Milan, who had led her to Christ over a decade earlier. She took up her pen and began to write. Before the morning was over, she had written the beautiful hymn we have all come to know and love, "Just as I Am."[185]

FRANCES RIDLEY HAVERGAL (1836–1879)

This gifted poetess and hymn-writer was born in 1836 into the home of a rector where Christ was honoured and served, in the Church of England. When she was eleven years of age, her mother died, but three years later she was led to Christ by her stepmother. She experienced ill health most of her life and died in her early forties, but she has become known through her writings as having had a deep and meaningful walk with her Lord. Physically weak, she grew increasingly spiritually strong.

Frances wrote her first hymn a short while after her twenty-first birthday while visiting the home of a minister in Germany. She found there an inscription

---

[183] Ibid., 254.
[184] Ibid., 284.
[185] Kenneth W. Osbeck, *101 Hymn Stories: The Inspiring True Stories Behind 101 Favorite Hymns* (Grand Rapids, MI: Kregel Publications, 1982), 146–148.

under a picture of the Lord Jesus, which read, "I did this for thee, what hast thou done for me?" As her tired body relaxed by the picture, she began to write the words to the hymn "I Gave My Life for Thee." She nearly threw the copy away, but in the end she crumpled up the paper and put it in her pocket. She later showed the words to her father, who set about to compose a tune for his daughter's writing.

Later that year, Frances was visiting in a country home for five days when she felt compelled to pray for everyone present. On the last night of her visit, the words of a hymn came to her as she lay awake at night. How many times we have sung this beautiful hymn with little thought of where it originated. The hymn she wrote was "Take My Life and Let It Be."

The last days for Frances were filled with great anguish and pain. Knowing her end was near, she requested that her favourite verse of Scripture be placed on her tombstone: *"the blood of Jesus Christ, His Son, cleanseth us from all sin"* (1 John 1:7, KJV).[186]

PERRY ROCKWOOD (1917–2008)

Perry Rockwood's voice filled the airwaves for over sixty years on *The People's Gospel Hour*. For many years, he was the pastor of Missionary Bible Church in Halifax, and he was for a time the pastor of St. James Presbyterian Church in Truro, Nova Scotia. He was also the founding pastor of the People's Church in Truro. His vibrant ministry included a well-stocked Bible bookstore in Halifax, as well as a monthly magazine, *The Gospel Standard*. He was well-known for his uncompromising stand for the King James Version of the Bible and remained active in ministry until several weeks before his passing in March 2008, just a few days from his ninety-first birthday. Pastor Rockwood's outreach ministry is still carried on by a faithful staff whose love for Christ and deep respect for their now departed pastor is abundantly evident.[187]

I have personally attended several of the annual Bible conferences sponsored by the Missionary Bible Church, where Pastor Rockwood and members of his staff, as well as guest speakers, filled the pulpit for eight days of meetings. The week always included a trip to Peggy's Cove, which was usually good-naturedly promoted by Pastor Rockwood. I was present at the 2007 conference and was simply amazed at the strength and vitality of this ninety-year-old preacher. At one of the evening services, he preached for over forty minutes with the enthusiasm

---

[186] Ibid., 239–241.

[187] Perry Rockwood, *Triumph in God: The Life Story of Radio Pastor Perry F. Rockwood* (Halifax, NS: The People's Gospel Hour), 7, 40–41.

and recall of a man half his age. If he had notes, I don't think he consulted them; instead he looked straight at his audience throughout the sermon. His speech was clear and he stood fully erect as he addressed the congregation, with the only hints of his advanced age being his white hair and a hearing aid.

Rockwood, who came from New Glasgow in Pictou County, Nova Scotia, took some of his early training at Acadia University, where he met his first wife, Ena. Many people are not aware that for a while the Rockwoods were unequally yoked. Not until they moved to Truro and her husband became pastor of the Presbyterian Church on Prince Street did Ena come to the realization that she was not a Christian. Following a time of sharing and prayer with her husband, she gave her heart to Christ.[188]

From Perry Rockwood's personal account, we learn that for many years there was no God in his home and no Bible. His life had no purpose and no meaning, and Rockwood shares that he had become totally dissatisfied. After numerous refusals on previous occasions, he accepted an invitation from a man boarding at his home to attend a church service in his area. It happened on that night to be an induction service at St. Andrews Presbyterian Church in New Glasgow. At the close of the service, the unhappy high school graduate made the acquaintance of Rev. William Ooms from Ohio. The visiting preacher made clear to Rockwood that the first step to understanding the Bible was to be born again. After sharing John 3:16 with the young man, Ooms led Rockwood to Christ. With deep gratitude, Rockwood never hid his deep admiration for the godly influence of Rev. & Mrs. Ooms on his life that special day in 1936.[189]

SHELLEY-ANN BROWN, OLYMPIC MEDALLIST

This young lady, born to Jamaican immigrant parents and raised in Pickering, Ontario, competed in the two-woman bobsled competition and took home the silver medal in the 2010 Winter Olympics in Vancouver. I asked Shelley-Ann about the relevancy of the Bible as well as the role of Christianity in her parents' homeland of Jamaica. I was impressed with her reply.

> Absolutely! Even though the Bible was written thousands of years ago and has a historical and cultural context, it was written for all people and for all generations. Just as I believe that God is the same yesterday, today and forever, so is His Word! In fact, the urgency of the message of the Bible increases with each passing day. The entirety of Scripture

---

[188] Ibid., 5–7.
[189] Ibid., 1.

from Genesis to Revelation is a beautiful and complex narrative with the singular message of God's redemptive plan for mankind through Jesus Christ; The Way, The Truth and the Life! From my standpoint, yes, Christianity plays a major role in Jamaican culture. I read once that Jamaica has more churches per capita than any other country. I am not certain if that particular statistic is still true, but I do know that Christianity has been very influential in shaping the culture of Jamaica. While, of course, there are Jamaicans of all walks and faiths, I have never met a Jamaican that did not have a belief in God.[190]

This Christian athlete counts her Olympic experience as one of the most momentous occasions of her life, but she is now focused on her future, which includes being the best teacher she can be. She sees her family and friends as blessings she did not orchestrate, and she relates all of her life to her salvation, which is completely unmerited and only possible through the awesome grace of God."[191]

This thrill-loving medallist has retired (for now), saying she's about sixty-five in athlete years, but she's not about to predict where God may lead her next. In her words,

God has filled my life so far with exciting adventures and interesting journeys complete with unknown twists and turns… It's better than any race or any bobsleigh ride I'd ever been on.[192]

We are all waiting to see where God takes this vibrant Christian athlete and teacher. When she is not travelling, Shelley-Ann attends Grace Christian Life Centre in Scarborough, Ontario.

[190] From an email message to the author. February 5, 2013.
[191] Ibid.
[192] Ibid.

CHAPTER NINE

Ancient Greece Goes Modern

It may come as an astounding fact to some that the key to understanding the destructive biblical criticism that reared its ugly head in the eighteenth and nineteenth centuries lies back in ancient Greece, hundreds of years before the time of Christ. The difficulties Christians face today in regard to the authority of the Bible can be traced to the pervading influence of a pagan philosophical culture in ancient Greece over 2,500 years ago. The church is in the world, and though not of it, she is affected by all that goes on around her. This is why Christians are urged to be vigilant, because the Devil is ever lurking around, seeking whom he may destroy (1 Peter 5:8).

These ancient philosophers were largely unchallenged until they were met with one of their own who ushered in a new era with emphasis on definition of terms, piety, courage, and justice. The teachings of Socrates mark the beginning of Greek moral philosophy, arguing that it is better to suffer injustice than to commit an injustice. He believed in one true God. In his mind, priority should be given to caring for one's soul. He rejected much of what we define now as fable and myth.

He never founded a school, wrote nothing down, and though having many admirers he had no formal disciples, yet he rose to become one of the most celebrated philosophers of the ancient world. He is remembered by many for the manner in which he died, being forced to drink the poisonous hemlock by the authorities of the time, who were offended by his teachings.[193]

His most notable follower was Plato, who in turn mentored Aristotle. These three men have made major impact on Western thought. Plato surely reflected his mentor when he speculated "that only a revelation from God could supply an adequate key to the mysteries of origin, purpose, and destiny."[194]

ATOMISM AND EVOLUTIONARY THEORY—ECHOES OF ANCIENT GREECE

The word atom, from the Greek word *atomos*, means "indivisible" and reminds us of the original Greek theory that this microscopic particle was incapable of being divided. The more recent theory, undergirded by experimental and scientific data, has ably demonstrated that the atom can indeed be divided. This was evidenced in the making of the atomic bomb that was unleashed with shocking destructive force in Japan in 1945. The atomic theory was held in ancient Greece by Democritus (460–362 BC), Empedocles (490–430 BC), and others.[195]

The philosophers who opposed Socrates spent their time on speculations about the world around them, skepticism, and critical analysis. They believed that nothing was certain truth, doubted everything, and weighed everything in the crucible of their fallen and finite minds. They were no strangers to atomic theory and believed in the concept of eternal materialism.[196] They also developed the theory of evolution thousands of years before Darwin, and the theory of long geologic ages before Lyell. All literature was submitted to their prejudiced, skeptical critical analysis. From a biblical perspective, this type of negative, detailed analysis had its roots at the very beginning of the human race when Satan questioned Eve about the words of her Creator in Genesis 3:1.

The Apostle Paul encountered some of these naturalists at Athens, as recorded in Acts 17:16–34. Their adoption of a pantheon of gods, combined with their rejection of a Designer-Creator, left Paul deeply moved (Acts 17:16) and prompted his famous sermon from Mars Hill (Acts 17:22–31). Descended from Greek philosophers who had preceded them over five hundred years earlier,

---

[193] Cowan and Guinness, *Invitation to the Classics*, 59–66.
[194] Merrill C. Tenney, *The Bible: The Living Word of Revelation* (Grand Rapids, MI: Zondervan Publishing House, 1975), 13.
[195] "Atom," *Encyclopaedia Britannica, Volume 2* (Toronto, ON: William Benton, 1961), 635.
[196] MacArthur, *The MacArthur Study Bible*, 1666. Note on Acts 17:18.

they were a proud and culture-minded bunch who were especially offended by Paul's emphasis on the resurrection of the dead, which was given no room in their speculations.

> Stoics. Like all other Greek and Roman philosophies of the day, Epicureanism and Stoicism were based on an evolutionary worldview. The Epicureans were essentially atheists, like modern Darwinists, whereas the Stoics were pantheists, much like modern New Age evolutionists. Both believed in an infinitely old universe, and both rejected the concept of an omnipotent transcendent Creator. On the popular level, both were expressed in terms of polytheism, astrology and spiritism with the mini gods and goddesses essentially being personifications of natural forces and systems. Both would naturally be strongly opposed to biblical creationist Christianity.[197]

The early church delivered a huge blow to these philosophic humanists from Greece. The doubts and deliberations of an uncertain mindset were no match for the authoritative teaching and preaching of God's Word, especially when some of their own submitted to the claims of Christ (Acts 17:34). This new teaching challenged the Greeks and their culture like no other before or since (Acts 17:18–21).

THE RENAISSANCE: REBIRTH OF PAGAN GREEK PHILOSOPHY

For a time, it seemed that the humanistic ruminations of a bygone era would be buried and forgotten forever, until around the eighth century and the reign of Emperor Charlemagne, when there was witnessed the birth pangs of a great literary and cultural movement which found its source in the philosophies of ancient Greece. Further signs came in the tenth century, with the accession of Emperor Otto I to be the head of the Roman Empire in the west (later called the Holy Roman Empire) in 962. The twelfth century witnessed the rediscovered works of Aristotle fusing with the teachings of Christianity to produce what is now known as scholasticism. It was the Italians, however, who, by revitalizing the arts, literature, and architecture of ancient Rome and Greece throughout the fourteenth through sixteenth centuries, gave birth to what is known as the Renaissance. This great revival of literary, cultural, and artistic expression that found its source in past humanistic societies gave mankind the centre of

---

[197] Morris, *The Henry Morris Study Bible*, 1671.

attention and glorified man's intellectual pursuits. Some would capably argue that the Renaissance is still very much alive and flourishing in our time.[198]

The scientific revolution of the seventeenth century fed off the burning embers of Renaissance thinking. This was followed by the Enlightenment of the eighteenth century, which was carried along by the same comparisons, criticisms, and acute analysis that was evident in ancient Greece.

> The word *renaissance* means a new birth or revival. The Renaissance is a revival of arts and letters, under classical influence, marking the transition from the Middle Ages to the modern world; period of this revival beginning in the 14th century in Italy and lasting into the 17th century. A Renaissance man is a person who has wide interest and is expert in several areas.[199]

One of the more influential spokesmen for the great rebirth and revival of long ago philosophers was Thomas More, an astute Roman Catholic from Great Britain who was beheaded on orders from King Henry VIII in 1535 for his refusal to recognize England's king as the head of the church. Though removed from our time by nearly five hundred years, this politician and scholar helped to create the mindset and culture of our modern era. Nineteen years before his death, Thomas More wrote his *Utopia*, a Latin masterpiece that was translated into English in 1556. In this humanistic satire, a society living on an isolated island struggles with the stresses of living together and seeks to produce the ideal conditions for a stable and prosperous community that is beneficial to all concerned.

Cowan and Guinness explain, "More lived during the Renaissance when a fresh awareness of the philosophic and artistic triumphs of classical Greece and Rome led to fresh efforts to perfect the human condition."[200] Using the backdrop of such writings as those of Plato, the writer of *Utopia* fully represented Renaissance awareness by providing an arena of possibility to solve the problems of mankind by introducing new and imaginative political and social orders.

The humanistic approach that gave life and movement to the Renaissance was taken to its most extreme parameters by the German mystic, Meister Eckhart (1260–1327), who blatantly suggested that humanity was divine, leaving no room

[198] Una McGovern, ed., "Renaissance," *Chambers Dictionary of World History* (Edinburgh, UK: Chambers Harrap Publishers, 2005), 743–744.
[199] "Renaissance," *Webster's English Dictionary* (New Lanark, Scotland: Geddes and Grosset, 2001), 316.
[200] Cowan and Guinness, *Invitation to the Classics*, 117–120.

for any God separate from mankind.[201] Some of the great political and social movements of the modern era have been sadistic and brutal in their attempts to cure the ills of society without God and divorced from the Judeo-Christian ethic presented in the Scriptures. Hitler's final solution saw the murder of six million Jews in death camps in his futile attempt to produce the perfect race.[202] Using the thoughts of writers such as Karl Marx (who wrote the *Communist Manifesto* in 1848), Lenin and Stalin led Russia into many decades of atheistic communism. In Russia alone, many millions of human beings were murdered by a communist killing machine that was supposedly designed to improve the human condition worldwide. Instead of a panacea for societal ills, communism became a living nightmare. David Marshall describes the scene in chilling fashion:

> On an *average* wintry day of Stalin's 25-year reign, he and his comrades processed more souls across the River Styx than were killed in *three centuries* of the Spanish Inquisition, from Argentina to Andalucía."[203]

BIBLICAL CRITICISM: A SANITIZED VERSION OF GREEK PHILOSOPHY

A straight line can now be drawn from ancient Greece to the Renaissance. The line continues into the eighteenth and nineteenth centuries, when there developed a new approach to God's Word that is now referred to as biblical criticism, or the historical-critical method. The theological world, already weakened by centuries of humanism, was shaken by a theory of human origins that offered a challenge to divine revelation and, more particularly, the Genesis account of creation.

DARWIN AND LYELL

One only has to review the older commentaries that were published in the mid-nineteenth century to see how Bible believers were scurrying around in an effort to refute the not-so-new teachings of Charles Darwin, which seemed to present an ironclad argument against the biblical account of human origin. To further the cause of naturalism, Scottish geologist Charles Lyell proposed that long geologic ages spanned billions of years and that changes took place gradually over time. He taught that things have continued as they were to the present time and left no room for catastrophism such as the flood of Genesis. Lyell's teaching is now referred to as uniformitarianism.[204]

---

[201] Ibid., 215.

[202] "Adolf Hitler," *Chambers Dictionary of World History*, 395.

[203] Marshall, *The Truth Behind the New Atheism*, 190.

[204] Kevin Logan, *Responding to the Challenge of Evolution* (Paris, ON: Cook Communications, 2005), 35, 75–76.

As Renaissance thinking found its way into the halls of learning, it began to affect the theological views of professors in Christian institutes as well. The theistic and biblical foundations of the Protestant Reformation were gradually weakened by the naturalism of the Renaissance. By the eighteenth century, a new approach was taken to the Bible by which the Word of God, rather than being seen as divine revelation, was subject to the critical analysis of learned individuals who began to treat the Bible with the same regard as any other book.

Paul Tournier gives us a vivid insight into the direction that mankind was heading in the early part of the seventeenth century as he references Rene Descartes, the French philosopher who is considered the father of modern philosophy:

> The modern world had honestly decided to exclude everything emotional, moral, and religious. On November 10, 1619, in the course of a real mystical crisis, Descartes caught a glimpse of a new civilization in which men, in order to be able to tolerate themselves, would establish a science founded upon reason and common sense, a dependable science free from those moral value judgments which in his convictions had been the cause of all their previous controversies.[205]

Without a moral code such as the Ten Commandments, man would then be freed from moral strictures and any supposed responsibility to a divine Creator. Does this not sound like the state of affairs in our own time? To ask the question is to answer it.

Feeding off the still burning embers of the Renaissance, two significant thought patterns emerged in the eighteenth and nineteenth centuries that have found their way into evangelical Christianity. The first supposition that raised doubts about the truth of Scripture was that there is more than one perspective within its pages, thus creating literary, historical, and theological differences. The second supposition was that some ancient writings outside the Bible are sometimes similar to Scripture, suggesting a common source. Both of these have been capably dealt with by God-fearing scholars whose detailed research has proven that these supposed arguments against biblical truth are built on a foundation of sand. Many of the assumed differences within the Bible actually complement each other rather than contradict each other, giving balance and

---

[205] Lindsell, *The Bible in the Balance*, 277.

stability to biblical truth. It has also been shown that the vast majority of non-biblical writings are far removed from God's revelation in the Scriptures.[206]

The following quote from John Hayes is designed to tone down the implications of the critical approach to Scripture:

> The term "criticism" here does not imply faultfinding or a disapproving judgment; rather, it refers to a careful, systematic, open-minded examination of the documents in an attempt to learn all that can be learned about and from them.
>
> The basic presupposition of biblical criticism is that the Bible, whatever else it may be, is a collection of human documents written by human authors in human language and therefore subject to the same canons of historical and literary investigation as all other books. In other words, the Bible is to be read and studied in exactly the same way as any other collection of ancient documents. This means that one should not approach the Bible with any preconceived ideas about its origin, nature, content, meaning, or relevance for today, but rather should form opinions on these matters only after a careful study of the Biblical materials themselves.[207]

Harold Lindsell comes to the following conclusion concerning the historical-critical take on the Bible: "The historical-critical method humanizes the Bible while it downgrades the divine authorship... Worst of all... it makes the Bible a closed book to the common man."[208] The so-called experts place the truth of God's Word under the ever-doubtful scrutiny of human wisdom and inevitably come out on the wrong side of scriptural truth. The key issue is one of authority, and among the evangelicals of today there is increasing pressure to sacrifice the tenets of Scripture on the altar of human expediency and unbelief.

The Renaissance was the link between ancient Greek philosophy and the biblical criticism that found its way into the higher intellectual echelons of evangelical scholarship and has ever since created major havoc among those who have embraced the Bible as a direct revelation from God Himself. The critical and skeptical analysis that was so common in ancient Greece, and found ready acceptance by generations of human beings throughout the Renaissance

[206] John H. Hayes, *Introduction to the Bible* (Peabody, MA: Prince Press/Hendrickson, 1971), 10–11.
[207] Ibid., 11.
[208] Lindsell, *The Bible in the Balance*, 300–301.

period, now found a point of contact in the great religious seminaries of Europe, especially in Germany, where even stalwart Bible scholars became fascinated with a philosophy that came disguised as a reasonable, common sense approach to the Word of God.[209] Theological students from Great Britain and North America were infected by this humanistic virus as they flocked to the religious universities of Germany to further their theological studies. How could the country that gave us Martin Luther and provided the impetus for the Protestant Reformation find itself so far removed from the tenets of a movement that shook the Roman Catholic Church to its foundations and drew its very breath from the truth of Scripture?[210]

Reflecting again on Paul's visit to Athens in Acts 17, there is a fascinating parallel with another visitor who was tried and condemned in this same place many years earlier:

> The debates in the market-place led to more misunderstanding than enlightenment. At best Paul was regarded as a babbler, or more literally someone who collects scraps, since they would have found echoes of bits and pieces of their systems in his beliefs. At worst Paul was accused of a serious crime; advocating foreign gods… the very crime of which the great philosopher Socrates had been accused, also in Athens 450 years earlier, and which led to his death.[211]

Like the philosophers in the book of Acts who questioned and scrutinized the words of the apostle Paul, modern-day critics approach the Bible the exact same way. No longer truth to be acknowledged and acted upon, the Scriptures are subject to a third-degree treatment that sees every event, person, and truth open to the destructive criticism of a Renaissance remnant determined to judge God's truth on the basis of humanistic reasoning. We will never know how many souls have been lost and how many Christians have been left confused and shattered by this insidious enemy of God's truth.

Here is one example of a student whose faith was destroyed by a Christian college that had obviously abandoned the inerrancy of Scripture.

> She enters a class in biblical history. One by one she sees them go— the facts which to her were the very foundations of her religious life.

---

[209] Lindsell, *The Battle for the Bible*, 95, 185–186, 188–192.

[210] Lindsell, *The Bible in the Balance*, 279–280.

[211] D.A. Carson, R.T. France, and Jan Moatyer, *New Bible Commentary* (Downers Grove, IL: Intervarsity Press, 2007, 1093.

She can no longer believe in the creation of the world as told in the Old Testament or in the story of Moses and the burning bush. As she goes on into the study of the New Testament higher criticism lays bare to her the fact that the story of Jesus' birth is not authenticated, that the feeding of the five thousand and Christ's walking on the sea cannot be taken literally and that possibly even her belief in the Resurrection is groundless. In fact all the mysterious and supernatural gifts of Jesus which had formed the core of her spiritual life now seem either based on unhistorical facts or disapproved by the workings of natural laws... Her loss of faith in everything divine first stuns her but leaves her, at last, as she styles herself, "a regretful agnostic."[212]

Stripped of its divine authority, the Bible was left only a shell of its former self. The battle continues to this present day, as more and more churches and theological schools fall victim to historical-criticism, relegating God's precious Word to the scrapheap of philosophical speculation and distorting the Scriptures to their own destruction (2 Peter 3:16). The critical method of biblical investigation is easily tracked to the Renaissance and is a throwback to the literature and art of the ancient Greeks and Romans. A further quote from the scholarly but admittedly liberal theologian John H. Hayes brings it all into clear perspective:

Until modern times, the popular belief was that, whoever may have written the actual words, the real author of the Bible was the Spirit of God, who had spoken through the various authors. This doctrine of divine inspiration implied infallibility, and so the Bible was regarded as in a very literal sense the Word of God. Beginning with the Renaissance, however, and particularly during the Enlightenment, men began to question many things, including the idea of a divinely dictated sacred book.[213]

Timeframes for the prophetical writings of men like Isaiah and Daniel are purposely changed to explain away fulfilled prophecies. The Bible is considered to be imbedded in a past culture, which means that at least some of its teachings cannot be applied to our more "enlightened" culture of today.

---

[212] Lindsell, *The Bible in the Balance*, 328.
[213] Hayes, *Introduction to the Bible*, 10.

The blood atonement is considered to be a relic from the past that presents an embarrassment to today's more refined approach to the basis of our salvation. Increasing multiculturalism in our society has led to a weakening of the biblical teaching about Jesus being the only way to heaven. The subject of eternal hell is hardly mentioned in many of our evangelical churches any more, which causes us to wonder whether we any longer accept the biblical teaching on this unpopular doctrine.[214]

THE FATHER OF HISTORICAL-CRITICISM

Harold Lindsell reminds us that the man who is generally regarded as the father of the historical-critical approach to the Scripture was born into the home of a Lutheran pietist pastor. Denying the orthodoxy of his father, as well as the verbal inspiration of the Scriptures, he firmly held to an interpretation of the Bible that was strictly historical and rejected God's supernatural activity in history. Accepting that the Bible contained the Word of God but that not all of Scripture was the Word of God, Johann Salomo Semler (1725–1791) openly confessed his total rejection of Reformation teaching as well as that of Augustine. Lindsell writes of him that he is

> usually designated as father of the technique which not only handled the Bible as an object for historical scrutiny and criticism, but also as a book little different from and no more holy than any other, and surely not to be equated with the Word of God. Very plainly he was saying that he rejected the divine inspiration of the text.[215]

Perfectly aligned with ancient Greek philosophy and given acceptance and sophistication by the Renaissance, Semler's views were readily received by theologians of his day and, amazingly, are now being received by evangelical Christendom, which should have been the first to reject his liberal approach. Lindsell gives this cogent assessment of historical-criticism as represented by Semler and others of his calibre.

At the heart of the historical-critical method lies the notion that the Bible is subject to something outside of it and this becomes superior to Scripture.[216]

In other words, God and His Word are to be cast aside in order for man's wisdom to have centre stage, as was the case in ancient Greece.

---

[214] Lindsell, *The Bible in the Balance*, 151, 157, 159, 289, 294–295, 358.
[215] Ibid., 280–281.
[216] Ibid., 284.

WE MUST CHOOSE

There are at least four issues that make for much heated and politically charged discussion in our day. These are all dealt with in the Scriptures and we name them here:

- The issue of homosexuality.
- The issue of creation versus evolution.
- The issue of the distinctive roles of men and women.
- The issue of eternal punishment.

Without going into the fine details, let me just say that our North American culture is not going to accept the biblical approach to any of these issues. But the Christian can only make one choice—we must accept the biblical teaching in these areas and choose the authority of the Bible. The Bible is not bound to our culture or to the opinions of mere humans. The fact that these sensitive and emotional issues are being hotly debated among even those who claim to embrace and support the Word of God is a great tragedy of our time.

Perhaps the most significant issue that has eroded confidence in the integrity of the Bible is the theory of evolution. The assertion that the Earth and all living things came into being as a result of random chance, an accidental process, rather than a creative act of God demands an answer from Bible believers. Henry M. Morris III can help us here:

In order for evolutionary scientists to demonstrate that simple life forms have changed into more complex life forms, over time, they must demonstrate it historically and by producing examples of such changes… then there ought to be many, many transitional remains available for scientists to uncover and observe in the fossil record.[217]

Amazingly, to our knowledge, none have ever been found.

Ever since Charles Darwin's 1859 publication of *The Origin of Species*, many Christians have felt compelled to go on the defensive. Dr. Nigel Cameron observes,

[How] quickly theologians and biblical commentators abandoned the traditional interpretation of Genesis in order to be accepted by

---

[217] Henry Morris III, *5 Reasons to Believe in Recent Creation* (Dallas, TX: Institute for Creation Researches, 2008), 21.

the burgeoning "scientific" consensus of the late 19th and early 20th centuries.[218]

The catastrophic flood recorded in Genesis 6–9 presents yet another magnet for fierce debate. From the Scriptures, we learn of a massive wall of water that fully enveloped the planet at some time in the ancient past. Skeptics deny that such a catastrophic event ever took place. Some Christians are convinced of a localized event rather than a worldwide deluge. As Tas Walker comments,

> If the flood were local, why did Noah have to build a gigantic Ark? He could have walked to the other side of the mountain and escaped. Why put birds on board? They could have flown away.[219]

The report of the universal flood can be found in over two hundred accounts, from both ancient and present cultural settings. From documents left from the Assyrian King Ashur Banipal, we learn of a great worldwide flood. Fossils have been found on the top of Mount Everest including fish bones and clam shells. There is also evidence of fossils being laid down in sediments left by fast-moving water.[220]

The real issue, above all else, is the authority of the Bible. We must be convinced of the truth of Scripture and not throw the precious Bible into the trash bin of humanistic speculations, naturalistic theories, manmade agendas, or cultural prejudices. We must refuse to trust our eternal well-being with any authority or agenda that lies outside of biblical revelation.

Within today's evangelical churches, denominations, and parachurch groups there are pockets of resistance to an infallible Bible. The abandonment of biblical inerrancy leads inevitably to theological deterioration and apostasy. There is no middle ground here. The Bible is either fully inerrant or rife with numerous errors. The following comment from Harold Lindsell leaves no room for a neutral position on biblical accuracy: "Errancy and inerrancy constitute the two principles and which one a person chooses determines where he will end up."[221] The Bible is indeed our greatest treasure!

[218] Jonathan Sarfati, *Refuting Compromise* (Green Forest, AR: Master Books, 2004), 9.
[219] Tas Walker, *The Genesis Flood: Fact or Fiction?* (Brisbane, Australia: Creation Ministries International, 2007), 12.
[220] Dave Balsiger and Charles Sellier Jr., *In Search of Noah's Ark* (Los Angeles, CA: Sun Classic Books, 1976), 5, 27, 31, 43.
[221] Lindsell, *The Battle for the Bible*, 142.

CHAPTER TEN

The Testimony of Scripture

The English Bible is comprised of 1,189 chapters, 31,173 verses, and 774,746 words, which, due to the massive material it covers, opens itself to intricate scrutiny and endless questioning. Interestingly enough, one of the most enlightening avenues of approach to biblical trustworthiness is what the Bible says about itself.[222]

From Genesis to Revelation, the Bible lays claim to divine origin. Over two thousand times in the Old Testament alone, the Scriptures claim to be the Word of God. Over forty times in the New Testament, the expression "the Word of God" is to be found. Whether we are looking at the words of Christ, or Luke, or the apostle Paul, they all treat their words as Holy Writ. Psalm 19, Psalm 119, Proverbs 30:5–6, and 2 Timothy 3:15 all make powerful statements about the Word of God. Another verse that speaks of the ever-present influence of its words is found in Isaiah 55:11:

> So shall My word be that goes forth from My mouth; it shall not return to Me void, but it shall accomplish what I please, and it shall prosper in the thing for which I sent it. (NKJV)

---

[222] John MacArthur, "How We Got the Bible," *The MacArthur Study Bible, New King James Version* (Nashville, TN: Word Publishing, 1997), xiii.

The ongoing question that is often asked is how to validate what book or books are part of God's revelation as opposed to those that are not. John MacArthur offers what appears to be the most conclusive answer:

> First, the writing had to have a recognized prophet or apostle as its author (or one associated with them, as in the case of Mark, Luke, Hebrews, James, and Jude). Second, the writing could not disagree with or contradict previous Scripture. Third, the writing had to have general consensus by the church as an inspired book.[223]

Over the centuries, these three principles were always used to validate the sacred writings. These same principles were also used to examine any book or writing claiming to be a part of the canon of Scripture.[224]

Based on these three principles, the fourteen books of the Apocrypha have been consistently rejected as Scripture by all but the Roman Catholic Church.[225] These mysterious writings are a convoluted mixture of history and myth that were a part of the early English translations, including the Geneva Bible of 1560 and the English version put out in 1611 by the King James translators. Though contained in the Septuagint, a Greek translation of the Old Testament Scriptures, they are never quoted or referred to by the Lord Jesus or any New Testament writer. Based on the three principles previously given, the New Testament books have been accepted as inspired since around 400 A.D.

> The term apocrypha [means] "hidden" [and] is a technical term concerning the revelation of certain books to the OT Canon, signifying that, while they are not approved for public lection, they are nevertheless valued for private study and edification… Christian usage and opinion about their status were somewhat ambiguous until the 16th century when twelve works were included in the Canon of the Roman Church by the Council of Trent; but Protestant thought (eg. Luther and the Anglican Church in the Thirty-Nine Articles) admitted them only for private edification.[226]

---

[223] Ibid., xiv.
[224] The word "canon" comes from the Greek word *kanon*, which refers to a reed. It is also a standard Hebrew unit of measure.
[225] Douglas, ed., "Apocrypha," *The New Bible Dictionary*, 55.
[226] Ibid.

These words come from the fourth-century theologian Cyril of Jerusalem (315–386). This Middle Eastern Christian ecclesiastic was several times the Bishop of Jerusalem.[227]

> In regard to the divine and holy mysteries of the faith, not the least part may be handed on without the Holy Scriptures. Do not be led astray by winning words and clever arguments. Even to me, who tell you these things, do not give ready belief, unless you receive from the Holy Scriptures the proof of the things which I announce. The salvation in which we believe is not proved from clever reasoning, but from the Holy Scriptures.[228]

Cyril lived at a time of great controversy concerning the canon of Scripture. There was heated discussion, often divisive, in regard to the apocryphal books, which are still accepted as Scripture by the Roman Catholic Church. Siding with men such as Jerome, Cyril made his position clear about these extra books. Along with men such as Athanasius, he maintained that these deuterocanonical books should be relegated to a subordinate position outside the canon proper. Cyril was quite uncompromising; books not in the public canon were not to be studied even in private.[229]

Many of the early church fathers, including Cyril of Jerusalem, had settled the issue of the canon and accepted only the sixty-six books that Protestants embrace today as being inspired and authoritative. Protestants in general do not accept the apocryphal works, the Nag Hammadi documents, or church tradition as having any authority in teaching or practice. The very best source for verifying Scripture that is divinely inspired is the Bible itself.

> It is the constant claim of the writers of Holy Writ that what they write is the authoritative and living Word of God. When the Old Testament is quoted in the New, statements like "God says" and "the Holy Spirit says" are frequent (e.g. Acts 1:16; 3:24–25; 2 Corinthians 6:16). What "the Scripture says" and what "God says" are quite simply the same thing in case after case. The Scripture is even personified as if it were God (cf. Galatians 3:8; Romans 9:17)… The phrase "It is written" (gegraptai), used often in the New Testament, settles the matter beyond reasonable

---

[227] McGovern, "Cyril of Alexandria," *Chambers Biographical Dictionary*, 387.

[228] Don Kistler, ed., *Sola Scriptura!* (Morgan, PA: Soli Deo Gloria Publications, 2000), 27.

[229] J.N.D. Kelly, *Early Christian Doctrines* (Peabody, MA: Prince Press/Hendrickson, 2004), 54–55.

doubt. When we come to the New Testament writings we immediately note that nothing less than the authority of the Old Testament Scriptures is ascribed to the writers of the New Testament (cf. Romans 1:15; 1 Timothy 2:7; Galatians 1:8,9; 1 Thessalonians 2:13). Gegraptai is used of New Testament writings and the apostolic text is placed on a par with the writings of the Old Testament (cf. 2 Peter 3:15, 16; Revelation 1:3)… The authority of the Scripture then, is not located in human brilliance or witness. It is not found in the person of Moses, Paul or Peter. The authority is found in the sovereign God Himself. The God who "breathed out" the words through human writers stands behind every statement, every doctrine, every promise and every command written in the Scripture.[230]

Over the years, some have attempted to add further writings to the sixty-six books that are now accepted as a completed document, the Bible. The Seventh-Day Adventists have given high priority to the writings of Ellen G. White, who in the introduction to *The Great Controversy Between Christ and Satan*, claims to be singularly gifted to see the truths of God's Word. The fact that she would strap us to the laws of the Old Testament (including Saturday worship) and claim that Sunday worshippers will receive the mark of the beast in a future time of tribulation is reason enough to reject any so-called authority in her writings. White became the leader of the Seventh-Day Adventist Church in 1863. Her followers embraced her teachings as the spirit of prophecy. She is reported to have "experienced during her lifetime two thousand visions and prophetic dreams."[231]

The Book of Mormon, given to us by Joseph Smith and the church he founded, claims an authority on par with the Scriptures. First published in 1830, these fifteen books are a strange mixture of Bible verses and fictional stories. Placing the Garden of Eden in North America rather than modern-day Iraq is just one example of the ludicrous claims contained in this book. The Mormons also speak of their ongoing struggle to be a god rather than worshipping the one true God.[232]

We know from students of biblical history that the Bible we hold in our hands has been remarkably preserved since the earliest writings. Our Lord knew

---

[230] Kistler, *Sola Scriptura!*, 96–98.
[231] McGovern, "Ellen Gould White," *Chambers Biographical Dictionary*, 1592.
[232] John R. Rice, *False Doctrines Answered from the Scriptures* (Murfreesboro, TN: Sword of the Lord Publishers, 1970), 361–363.

there would be continuing attacks on His Word, but He has promised in both testaments to preserve His Word (Isaiah 40:8, 1 Peter 1:25). The Word of God will be perpetuated even in heaven, according to Psalm 119:89. Our Lord Jesus gave His personal assurance that the very smallest detail of Scripture would be kept intact. This truth is brought to us in Matthew 5:18 and Luke 16:17. The Bible must be handled with care and respect at all times, and we are given due warning not to add or subtract from the sacred Scriptures (Revelation 22:18–19). C. Everett Koop states it well:

> With the completion of the canon of Scripture, the total revelation of God has been given (that is, not all that can be known about God, but all that God has decided to let us in on).[233]

Some go right outside the Bible, making statements that are obviously not based on the Scriptures.

> Presumptuous Christian writers claim to know God's intent, such as the author of the book that insists "God wants you well." So Who says so? Why should He want you well when He did not want the apostle Paul well?[234]

There is an abundance of so called "revelation" today. I am extremely cautious and suspicious of any ministry that appears to specialize in the "word of knowledge." Someone who claims to have the word of knowledge may address their television audience with words such as the following:

> "Someone in Topeka, Kansas, is right this moment being healed of a goiter." This is an astonishing thing. Here is a man hundreds of miles from the scene who is getting supernatural revelation of the healing of a specific disease in a specific city. What puzzles me is the restricted specificity of these revelations. The disease and the city are named, but never the name and address of the person being healed. Here the prophecy can be neither verified nor falsified.[235]

---

[233] Michael Horton, ed., *The Agony of Deceit* (Chicago, IL: Moody Press, 1990), 175.

[234] Ibid., 174.

[235] Don Kistler, ed. *Sola Scriptura: The Protestant Position on the Bible* (Morgan, PA: Soli Deo Gloria Publications, 2000), 90–91.

None of this has any authority and it is far removed from what we accept as inspired Scripture. The real need today is for Christians to read and study all of the Bible. Both testaments need to be appreciated for what they are—the pure and unadulterated Word of the Living God. Like Cyril of Jerusalem, we should accept nothing as authority except that which is found in the Bible. The words of any man or woman, including the words of this book you are now reading, should be tested in the crucible of the inspired Scripture to be certain we are in sync with the Word of God. The Bible is ever our very best resource for knowledge and instruction. Our sole resource for authority is the Bible.

Now these Jews were more noble than those in Thessalonica; they received the word with all eagerness, examining the Scripture daily to see if these things were so. (Acts 17:11, ESV)

ROBERT DICK WILSON, DEFENDER OF BIBLICAL AUTHORITY

One of the most astute students of the Scriptures was Robert Dick Wilson, who died in the early part of the twentieth century. This graduate of Princeton, who had received both his M.A. and Ph.D., was a staunch and able defender of biblical authority. In order to thoroughly study the Word of God, he mastered no less than forty-five ancient languages and dialects. He not only studied the Scriptures but numerous other ancient writings in their language of origin. He proved beyond doubt that only the Bible could be relied upon to be accurate in every detail while other accounts are full of error and fabrication.[236]

Wilson's research covered both testaments. He noted that while the Old Testament Scriptures are constantly vilified by the critics, they are fully sanctioned by the Lord Jesus Christ in the New Testament canon. In an obvious reference to the Old Testament Scriptures, the Lord Jesus Christ, who is the faithful and true witness (Revelation 3:14), declared without reservation, *"For verily I say unto you, Till heaven and earth pass, one jot or one title shall in no wise pass from the law, till all be fulfilled"* (Matthew 5:18, KJV).

He further stated in John 10:35 that *"the scripture cannot be broken"* (KJV). Wilson then takes us to the conclusion, which is clearly evident from the very words of Christ.

The history of the preparation of the world for the Gospel as set forth in the Old Testament is simple and clear and in the light of the New

---

[236] Wilmington, *Wilmington's Guide to the Bible*, 813–814.

Testament eminently reasonable. In fact, it has been considered so reasonable, so harmonious with what was to have been expected, that Christ and the apostles seem never to have doubted its veracity, and the Christian Church which they founded has been up to our times accepted it as fully consonant with the facts.[237]

Christ viewed the Old Testament as an authority without question and beyond discussion. So affirmative are the words of Christ concerning the Old Testament Scriptures that not trusting them would mean not trusting the words of our Saviour.

Wilson determined to learn Hebrew by heart, which he did. He also taught himself to read the New Testament in at least nine different languages. Following his graduation from seminary, he went to Germany. Knowing his professors were sceptical about the accuracy and truthfulness of Scripture, he determined to prove them wrong.

> After I had learned the necessary languages I set about the investigation of every consonant in the Hebrew Old Testament. There are about a million and a quarter of these; and it took me many years to achieve my task. I had to read the Old Testament through and look at every consonant in it; I had also to observe the variations of the text, as far as they were to be found in the manuscripts, or in the notes of the Massoretes (the Massoretes were a body of Jewish scholars who made it their business to hand down what they believed to be the true text of the Old Testament), or in the various versions, or in the parallel passages, or in the conjectural emendations of critics; and then I had to classify the results. I prize this form of textual research very highly; for my plan has been to reduce the Old Testament criticism to an absolutely objective science; something which is based on evidence, and not on opinion. I scarcely ever make a statement which rests merely on my own subjective belief.[238]

The writer then points out that Bible history and doctrine can only be fully appreciated after we have determined the true underlying text of the Hebrew. Wilson's research strengthened his confidence in God's Word.

---

[237] David Otis Fuller, ed., *Which Bible?* (Grand Rapids, MI: Grand Rapids International Publications, 1984), 50.
[238] Ibid., 44.

We can be absolutely certain that substantially we have the text of the Old Testament that Christ and the apostles had, and which was in existence from the beginning. I would like to give a few other examples of true Biblical criticism. I can remember when it was thought very unprofitable to read the long genealogies found in the first chapters of First Chronicles— nine chapters of proper names. But today, in the scientific criticism of the Old Testament, proper names are of the profoundest importance. The way in which they are written—indeed, all that is connected with them—has come to be one of the very foundations upon which scientific criticism of the Old Testament is built.

Take the following case. There are twenty-nine ancient kings whose names are mentioned not only in the Bible but also on monuments of their own time; many of them under their own supervision. There are one hundred and ninety-five consonants in these twenty-nine proper names. Yet we find that in the documents of the Hebrew Old Testament there are only two or three out of the entire hundred and ninety-five about which there can be any question of their being written in exactly the same way as they were inscribed on their own monuments. Some of these go back for two thousand years, some for four thousand; and are so written that every letter is clear and correct. This is surely a wonder.[239]

Wilson discovered that the classical writings, in their attempt to provide a register of kings for ancient civilizations, were often deficient in regard to spelling and chronology. (He found the biblical account both precise and refreshing.)

There are twenty-nine kings of Egypt, Israel, Moab, Damascus, Tyre, Babylon, Assyria, and Persia, referred to, and ten different countries among these twenty-nine; all of which are included in the Bible accounts and those of the monuments. Every one of these is given his right name in the Bible, his right country, and placed in the correct chronological order. Think what that means![240]

PAST AND PRESENT

What is history? Put very simply, history is a statement of what has happened. There are two tasks that weigh upon the serious student of history. The first is to reconstruct past events in a detailed and accurate manner. The passage of time

[239] Ibid., 44–45.
[240] Ibid., 46.

and lack of original sources presents a daunting task to the historian who desires to be true to the facts. The second task is to provide significance and meaning to the events of the past.

Many individuals have a very negative reaction to history, which, to them, brings up images of that which is old, boring, and insignificant. Not only is this a common response to secular history, but, sadly, this attitude often prevails in regard to biblical history as well. This must be faced squarely by the child of God. The Bible is a series of narratives and stories packed into sixty-six books, and they are all interconnected to give us the entire revelation that God wanted us to have. Whether we are speaking of the creation account in Genesis, the experiences of the Israelites in such books as Kings and Chronicles, the preaching of the prophets such as Jeremiah or Isaiah, or the events relating to the earthly ministry of the Lord Jesus Christ, they are all true, significant, and important.

> We are not to be afraid of any criticism of the Bible. We are not to be frightened when we find a difficulty, no matter how unanswerable or how insurmountable it first appears to be. Thousands of men saw these same difficulties before we were born. The Bible has been God's rock upon which his people could stand through centuries of rigid examination and it is not likely to go down before that which we might be able to discover today. To one who is at all familiar with the history of the critical attacks on the Bible, the confidence of the modern destructive critic who thinks he is going to annihilate this Gibraltar seems simply amusing.[241]

C.H. Spurgeon was once told that his sermons all sounded alike. The great London preacher had a ready reply: "Yes. I take a text anywhere in the Bible and make a beeline to the cross."[242]

The one great theme that runs from Genesis to Revelation is the Lord Jesus Christ. It begins with Genesis 3:15, where the seed of the woman is consistently seen by avid Bible students as a prediction of the crucifixion and resurrection of Christ, bringing about the defeat of Satan. The Messiah is seen throughout the Scriptures and pictured in the account of Noah's ark, the tabernacle, the Old Testament sacrifices, and numerous prophecies. His earthly pilgrimage is featured in the four Gospels, and He is the heartbeat of the New Testament epistles, which repeatedly speak of His second coming.

---

[241] Criswell, *Why I Preach*, 60.
[242] Ibid., 114.

In the Revelation, the last book of the canon, the many symbols and visions focus on the redemption plan of Christ and His return to rule the earth in righteousness. Criswell summarizes this assessment with these cogent words: "The whole Bible either points to Christ in his first coming or to Christ in his second coming. The entire Bible presents Jesus our Saviour."[243]

There are difficulties in the Bible that can be solved or explained. These are not errors but challenges to the reader of the Bible.

> In A.D. 1800 the French Institute in Paris had issued a list of 82 errors in the Bible which they believed would destroy Christianity. Today not one of these so-called errors is received as such, for with new discoveries the difficulties have been cleared away... Errors are inconsistent with an infallible Bible but difficulties are not.[244]

There are to be found in the Louvre in Paris three and a half miles of science books. All of them are obsolete.

> In 1861 the French Academy of Science published a brochure of fifty-one "scientific facts" which supposedly contradicted the Bible. These were used by the atheists of that day in ridiculing Christians. Today all fifty-one of those facts are unacceptable to modern scientists.[245]

Dr. James Dwight Dana of Yale University, considered possibly the most eminent geologist in American history, once said these words to a graduating class:

> Young men! As you go out into the world to face scientific problems, remember that I, an old man who has known only science all his life long, say to you, that there is nothing truer in all the universe than the scientific statements contained in the Word of God![246]

Over the centuries, the Bible has been under unrelenting attack. Criswell sums it up this way:

---

[243] Ibid.
[244] Ibid., 59.
[245] Wilmington, *Guide to the Bible*, 819.
[246] Ibid.

Through the years the attack upon the Bible has continued. Every engine of destruction that human wisdom, human science, human philosophy, human wit, human satire, human force, and human brutality could bring to bear against it. Yet the Bible still stands![247]

The early church endured waves of vicious persecution from the Roman Empire. None was more cruel or repressive than that which came in 303 A.D. as a quartet of emperors ruled the vast territory of Roman domination. Encouraged by one of his co-emperors, Diocletian unleashed a reign of terror on the Christian community that would last for the better part of a decade. Christians were ordered to worship the ancient gods of Rome and to forfeit their Bibles. Their refusal to comply brought imprisonment, torture, and death. Perhaps the reason Diocletian had at first hesitated to exact such suffering on some of his own citizens is that his wife Prisca and their daughter Valeria were Christians. It is a testimony to the strong faith of our ancestors that they held fast, accepting ill treatment, and in some cases a martyr's crown (Hebrews 11:30–35), rather than deny their faith.[248]

The Roman Empire in the early part of the fourth century was at the zenith of its strength and power. From a small village on the Tiber River in Italy, Rome had grown in a millennium to embrace an empire that encompassed a full one-quarter of the planet. Traditionally founded by twin brothers Remus and Romulus in 753 B.C., the city drew its name from the latter. Much of its early history is clouded with legend and mysticism, including the fanciful fiction that the deified Romulus, founder and first king of Rome, was taken to Mars in a chariot. Kingly rule eventually gave way to republicanism under two governors, finally evolving into emperor rule initiated by Caesar Augustus (Octavian), the adopted son of Julius Caesar in 29 B.C. The first emperor was acclaimed as the Prince of Peace, but when another Prince of Peace came on the scene early in the present era, dying on a Roman cross and rising from the grave three days later, the slumbering empire was suddenly aroused.[249]

The determined Diocletian enacted a reign of terror against all Christians. He especially hated the Bible and ordered all copies to be put to the torch. Accessing the political and military might of the most powerful empire the world had ever witnessed, his stated purpose was to annihilate the entire Christian community.

---

[247] Criswell, *Why I Preach*, 103.

[248] González, *Story of Christianity, Volume 1*, 102–104.

[249] M. Carey and H.H. Scullard, *A History of Rome* (London, UK: The MacMillan Press Ltd., 1979), 37, 39, 62, 315.

It was quite possibly the most vicious assault on any book and the adherents of its teachings the world has ever seen. Enacting a number of edicts, the emperor put ever-increasing pressure on believers. All copies of the Scriptures were to be surrendered to the Roman authorities.

Christians were ordered to forsake their Christian faith and embrace the gods of Rome. Some recanted under torture but untold numbers accepted death rather than surrender their precious Scriptures. The Bible was a sacred document to these brave believers and they would not easily part with their greatest treasure. They valued the Bible more than their very lives, and myriads of them sealed their faith with their own blood.

The believers who suffered deprivation and death under the heel of Rome knew full well the practical implications of Hebrews 11:36–38. They joined a long line of God's people who endured every kind of humiliation, tribulation, and even death for their Christian faith.[250]

And others had trial of cruel mockings and scourgings, yea, moreover of bonds and imprisonment: they were stoned, they were sawn asunder, were tempted, were slain with the sword: they wandered about in sheepskins and goatskins; being destitute, afflicted, tormented; (of whom the world was not worthy:) they wandered in deserts, and in mountains, and in dens and caves of the earth. (Hebrews 11:36–38, KJV)

Diocletian concluded, with so much bloodshed and so many Bibles confiscated and burned, that he had surely won his battle with the Christian populace. As with every other effort to purge the land of Bibles and nullify Christian faith, his most strenuous efforts were in vain. Beaten, discouraged, and weary of his duties, he retired in early 305, leaving him free to garden and dabble in philosophy. His edicts against the Christians and their Bible remained in effect. The killing of Christians continued and many were sent into forced labour in the stone quarries. The Roman authorities were unable to break the strong resolve of these stalwart Christians. Believers were deported to other parts of the empire.

The lists of martyrs grew longer and longer, and there seemed to be no end in sight… many of the condemned began organizing new churches in their places of punishment.[251]

It became increasingly clear to the political leaders that their most severe measures did nothing to stop the spread of Christian faith. Believers refused to

[250] Criswell, *Why I Preach*, 102–103.
[251] González, *Story of Christianity, Volume 1*, 106.

sacrifice to the Roman gods and would rather die than surrender their sacred writings. For a time, the Roman government descended into chaos due to jealous rivalries at the top echelon. To further exacerbate the growing tension, there was disagreement on how to handle the issue of Christian faith. Even among other religious belief systems, there was growing disgust with the terrible bloodshed being exacted against their Christian neighbours. Suddenly, and without warning, the persecution came to an end.

One of the four emperors of the time was Galerius, who had ruled in concert with Diocletian and was instrumental in spurring Diocletian's oppression of Christians. Galerius was the leading force against believers following Diocletian's retirement, while his fellow emperors, including a man called Constantine, were less oppressive. In 323, Constantine would become the sole emperor of the Roman Empire after banishing all rivals.

As the calendar turned to 311, two realities were apparent in the city of Rome. Galerius was losing his battle with Christians and the ailing emperor was losing his struggle with life. He was stricken with a painful disease and perhaps suspected he was being judged by his Creator, as suggested by some of the Christians. Perhaps there was some influence from his Christian wife, Valeria, the daughter of Diocletian. Whatever the case, he changed his policy and signed an edict on April 30, 311, officially ending all persecution of Christians.

The edict makes for an interesting read. It was worded in such a way to save face for the Roman authorities. Galerius suggests that all had been done by them with good intentions. Nothing was said about the many lives needlessly snuffed out. There was a candid admission that the attempt to turn Christians back to their Roman gods and religious traditions had failed. The closing line was a solicitation for the Christians to pray for all citizens of the empire.[252]

Five days after he signed the edict to end Rome's last and most ambitious assault on the Bible and her Christian citizens, Galerius passed on.

Galerius died after an illness which he attributed to the God of the Christians whom he had mercilessly persecuted; a deathbed repentance resulted in an edict granting greater toleration to Christians, but not in his recovery.[253]

We will not speculate on whether or not the repentance of Galerius was genuine. We can only hope so. What we do know is that Galerius is part of a

[252] Ibid., 104–106.
[253] Cary and Scullard, *History of Rome*, 522.

significant number of political leaders who throughout history have used military force, torture, intimidation, and imprisonment to fuel their hateful vendetta against God, His followers, and the Bible.

> [While] history shows many famous "Bible haters" who later became "Bible lovers," it never records the opposite. To take this a step further, it can be shown that no evil and murderous dictator or tyrant in history was ever a friend of the Bible and that no good and wise leader was ever an enemy of God's Word. Thus to deny the authority of the Bible is to set oneself against practically every great leader in Western civilization. While it is true that this in itself constitutes no absolute proof of the Scriptures, it does, nevertheless, lend itself to Abraham Lincoln's famous proverb: "you can fool some of the people all the time, and all of the people some of the time, but you can't fool all of the people all of the time!"[254]

Adolf Hitler used both the press and politics to push his agenda. His campaign of hatred against the Jews took root before the opening of hostilities that ushered in the Second World War in 1939. Before the war was brought to an end, thirty million people perished. Twelve million of that number lost their lives

> far away from the battlefields, by mass shootings, in forced labour camps and in the gas ovens of Belsen, Auschwitz, Ravensbruck… not forgetting the indiscriminate torture and murder of many prisoners of war, or the uprooting and extermination of entire villages and communities.[255]

His autobiography and political statement was written in his 1925 book, *Mein Kampf* (My Struggle). His extreme hatred for Jews is well known, but that's only part of the story. Some will argue that he was more tolerant of Christianity, but history paints a much different picture.

> [Why] did the Nazis kill thousands of Polish priests? Why did Dachau become "the largest religious community in the world," as William O'Malley put it, with some 2,750 clergymen interned? How did a "solidly Catholic region like Bavaria… end up having no Catholic schools by 1939"? Why, in newly annexed territories, were children

[254] Wilmington, *Guide to the Bible*, 798.
[255] McGovern, "Adolf Hitler," *Chambers Biographical Dictionary*, 732–733.

and schoolteachers forbidden from belonging to a church? It surely must be clear to any honest observer that "Hitler hated Christianity and planned to destroy it when the time came, as he explained in private. If the New Atheists [or others] want to do the same, let them take a number."[256]

What David Marshall is suggesting in the content of this discussion is that all repressive regimes in the past who have had a hatred for God, His church, and His sacred Word have failed in their bid to rid the planet of God. Future efforts will surely fail as well. You will recall that even the apostle Paul, before his remarkable conversion (Acts 9:3–20), did all in his power to stamp out the church in its early stages. He was present at Stephen's death and fully agreed with the action taken (Acts 8:1). Following the experience on the Damascus road, Paul's energy was expended in building the church rather than destroying it.

Soviet leader Joseph Stalin is yet another example of hatred of God, His people, and the Bible. He became the dictator of Russia following the death of Lenin in 1924.

> From this point on until his death in the fifties [1953], Stalin instituted a "ban the Bible" purge from the U.S.S.R. such as had never been witnessed before. This miserable man literally attempted to wipe the Word of God and the God of the Word from the Russian minds. Did he succeed? A recent poll taken in Russia shows that today more people than ever believe in God and his Word.[257]

Stalin was responsible for establishing the Gulag (an acronym in the Russian language for the Main Directorate for Corrective Labor Camps). The system was expanded in 1929 to exploit the Soviet Union's natural resources in the Siberian tundra. These camps were occupied by children, businessmen, landowners, murderers, thieves, common criminals, women, and religious dissenters. Millions never survived the harsh conditions and were never heard from again.

> They were shipped to and from the camps in cattle cars and corralled behind towering barbed-wire fences into hovels pocked by filth and disease. With few resources, clothes, and tools, they faced extreme

---

[256] Marshall, *Truth Behind the New Atheism*, 168.
[257] Wilmington, *Guide to the Bible*, 813.

hunger and harsh sub-zero climates where even fog would freeze. The brutality they endured parallels the Holocaust.[258]

The world is still learning about the terrible atrocities that were inflicted on these innocent people, thanks to the writings of Aleksandr I. Solzhenitsyn, a former prisoner, and Anne Applebaum. So far as we know, a woman by the name of Margaret Werner is the only American woman who survived Stalin's Gulag. Her amazing thirty-year journey, including many years in the Siberian death camps, is told by her son Karl Tobien. Throughout her terrible ordeal, Margaret sensed the hand of God upon her even though at the time she was not a Christian. She testifies of pouring out her heart to God, feeling overwhelmed with conflicting emotions. She returned to America in the early sixties, but not until 1991 was her relationship to Christ firmly established. Here is her testimony, in her son's words.

> Though Margaret had been on a personal quest for God nearly all her life, throughout all her trials and troubles in Russia, seeing and realizing the hand of God in her life all along the way, it was in the fall of 1991 that she actually invited Christ into her life, establishing that relationship, making him Lord and Savior, sealing her eternal fate. On April 7, 1997, I found the lifeless shell of my mother's body slumped across her bathroom floor. She was gone.[259]

Margaret Werner's journey has a happy ending, proving that God was not in any way hindered by a regime that had made every effort to keep God out of Russia. Foolishly, Stalin had made the statement, "God must be out of Russia in five years."[260] Stalin has been gone for sixty years, but God has never left and continues to build His church. The intellectual Solzhenitsyn was greatly influenced by Christians who were incarcerated with him and eventually gave his heart to Christ.

> Stalin didn't kill alone. Lenin, Mao, Pol Pot, both Kims, Ho, Castro, Ceausescu and Honecker were also atheists. In one third of the world, Communist parties announced the death of God on billboards,

---

[258] Karl Tobien, *Dancing under the Red Star* (Colorado Springs, CO: Waterbrook Press, 2006), xiii–xiv.
[259] Ibid., 279, 336.
[260] Ibid., 7.

chalkboards, radio waves, and blank walls. Secret worship services in homes, forests, and caves were forcibly broken up, along with the faces of many who attended. Millions were tortured for Christ… They had rats driven into their cells, were made to drink urine for communion, or were put into the "carcer", (a cupboard with sides studded by steel spikes) for writing the name of Jesus on a cell wall.[261]

Clement of Alexandria said that "all truth is God's truth." When men and women reject truth, they reject the one who embodies truth, God.[262] Following an eight-year stretch in Stalin's horrid death camps, Solzhenitsyn gave this explanation for the Gulag: "Men have forgotten God."[263]

Some use the pen to attack the God of the Bible. In a nineteen-adjective diatribe, the author of *The God Delusion*, Richard Dawkins, does just that as he unabashedly takes on the Yahweh of the Old Testament. For the reader who has come to know the God of the Bible through a personal relationship with the Lord Jesus Christ, this can be a difficult read. Even for one who may not have necessarily crossed the threshold of faith as yet but has deep respect for God and His blessed Word, this can be a rough road to travel. The author of this paragraph cannot seem to find enough words to vent his wrath against God. Here it is, in all its ugliness:

> The God of the Old Testament is arguably the most unpleasant character in all fiction: jealous and proud of it; a petty, unjust unforgiving control-freak; a vindictive, bloodthirsty ethnic cleanser; a misogynistic, homophobic, racist, infanticidal, genocidal, filicidal, pestilential, megalomaniacal, sadomasochistic, capriciously malevolent bully.[264]

David Marshall comments that Dawkins had little patience with Marshall's book, *The Truth Behind the New Atheism*. The kindest words Dawkins had for the Old Testament God are "petty," "vindictive," and "unjust." The New Testament may prove to be even worse with its doctrine of eternal damnation. I will leave this with no further comment except to include this excellent summation from David Marshall:

---

[261] Marshall, *Truth Behind the New Atheism*, 197–198.
[262] Ibid., 208.
[263] Ibid., 200.
[264] Richard Dawkins, *The God Delusion* (New York, NY: Houghton Mifflin, 2008), 51.

If the Bible is so bad, it's a wonder there are so many Christians and that the Jewish people survived so long with such an albatross around their necks![265]

And further from Marshall:

The world's most famous book may be its most unusual. Written by dozens of authors in three languages over more than a millennia, the Bible has been translated (at least in part) into 2400 languages, read by billions of people, and influenced almost every person alive today in many ways… Christians see all 66 documents as (in some sense) one work, with one Author. Historians see it as the text that, more than any, has made our world. Is its author God or the devil? Or was an ad hoc team of Iron Age poets, mystics, and fishermen, entirely responsible for its contents? The Bible is called "holy" because millions think God had a hand in its production. It is read by yam farmers in New Guinea… ex-gangsters in Japan with flowers tattooed across their chests, AIDS patients in India, and congressmen in Washington, D.C. Christians in early Rome and the Soviet Union copied it by hand and risked death to keep it safe.[266]

BILLY GRAHAM'S PIVOTAL DECISION

The ministry of Billy Graham is known around the world. His ministry has impacted the lives of millions of people. His life and ministry have revolved around one book, the Bible. Consider this:

For example, no single evangelist has preached the gospel to more people in the entire scope of the Christian movement. Nor have more people responded positively to the gospel call from one man. Around the world he is known, respected, and loved. Having preached in more than 185 countries and territories, and preached to more than 210 million people in countless cultural settings, year after year polls recognize him as one of the ten most respected personalities in the world. He has been honored by governments, a myriad of organizations, not to mention multiple churches and countless people.[267]

[265] Marshall, *Truth Behind the New Atheism*, 96.
[266] Ibid., 95–96.
[267] Lewis A. Drummond, *The Evangelist* (Nashville, TN: Word Publishing/Thomas Nelson, 2001), xi–xii.

Billy Graham has not been immune to the attacks that have been levelled against the Bible. The doubts and skepticism swirling around him needed to be addressed as he stood on the threshold of an evangelistic career. He experienced a personal struggle with the important issue of biblical authority. As a young man, he knew he could only go to the pulpit to preach the gospel from a book he could trust, with full assurance that the Bible is what it says it is, and nothing less. Honesty demanded that his convictions about the Bible be fully settled before he addressed his listeners.

Here is his straight-from-the-shoulder recollection of those early days of ministry:

I believe it is not possible to understand everything in the Bible intellectually. One day some years ago I decided to accept the Scriptures by faith. There were problems I could not reason through. When I accepted the Bible as the authoritative Word of God—by faith—I found immediately that it became a flame in my hand. That flame began to melt away unbelief in the hearts of many people and to move them to decide for Christ.

The Word became a hammer, breaking up stony hearts and shaping men into the likeness of God. Did not God say, "I will make my words in thy mouth fire" (Jer. 5:14), and "Is not my word like as a fire? Saith the Lord; and like a hammer that breaketh the rock in pieces?" (Jer. 23:29)

I found that I could take a simple outline, then put a number of Scripture quotations under each point, and God would use it mightily to cause men to make full commitment to Christ. I found that I did not have to rely upon cleverness, oratory, psychological manipulation, apt illustrations, or striking quotations from famous men. I began to rely more and more upon Scripture itself and God blessed it. I am convinced through my travels and experience that people all over the world are hungry to hear the Word of God.[268]

Prior to the 1949 evangelistic crusade in Los Angeles, Graham's struggle became a major crisis in his life. His friend and fellow evangelist Charles Templeton was having personal doubts about the simplicity and veracity of the gospel message. He was obviously in turmoil and planned to continue his

---

[268] MacArthur, *Why I Believe the Bible*, 19–20.

education at Princeton Theological Seminary. Graham had graduated from Wheaton College and had considered further training as well, but his ministry was growing so quickly that he dismissed the idea. The Graham team was already coming together, including Cliff Barrows, Grady Wilson, and George Beverly Shea.

Things came to a head for the young evangelist in September 1949. Graham and Templeton were together at a retreat centre near Los Angeles, and both were invited to speak at a student conference held at the Forest Home, which had been established by Henrietta Mears of the Hollywood Presbyterian Church.

The two young evangelists debated together about the validity of the Bible, which only increased the conflict for Graham. Before leaving the retreat centre, Billy Graham went for a walk by himself in the pine forest that surrounds Forest Home. He found his way to the golf course at Temple Terrace, and on the eighteenth green he had a talk with God and settled the issue. His decision that night laid the foundation for his entire ministry. He made the choice to accept the Bible as the authoritative Word of God, unfettered from any further doubt or debate. His decision that night has stood him well in his lengthy and productive ministry. A bronze tablet now marks the spot where the young Billy Graham made his life-changing decision on September 25, 1949.[269]

God mightily blessed the meetings in Los Angeles as Graham freely preached the Bible with no further conflict. It was at these meetings that racehorse owner, radio star, big gambler, and heavy drinker Stuart Hamblin was soundly converted. His faithful wife Suzy had prayed for him for sixteen years and encouraged her husband to attend the Graham meetings. Following his conversion, Hamblin went on the radio and publicly shared his testimony, telling his listeners that he was done with tobacco and liquor and had given his heart to Christ. The racehorses would be sold, except one. He had become a Christian in the early hours of that morning after waking Graham with a phone call at 2:00 a.m. That same evening, following his testimony on the radio, he attended the evening service and walked the sawdust trail as Graham gave his invitation. He had already told his radio audience what he was going to do in order to publicly tell all in attendance that his life had been changed in spectacular fashion.

Hamblin's conversion was just one of many proofs that God will always bless His Word. Billy Graham had indeed made a good decision that would be evidenced by God's abundant blessing through many years of ministry.[270]

---

[269] Drummond, *The Canvas Cathedral*, 4–6.
[270] Ibid., 7–10.

So shall my word be that goeth forth out of my mouth: it shall not return unto me void, but it shall accomplish that which I please, and it shall prosper in the thing whereto I sent it. (Isaiah 55:11, KJV)

Billy Graham made the wonderful discovery that God's Word needs no defence. The Word of God is authoritative and can be safely trusted. The great preacher Charles Spurgeon said it well: "There is no need for you to defend a lion when he's being attacked. All you need to do is open the gate and let him out."[271]

---

[271] MacArthur, *Why I Believe the Bible*, 20.

CONCLUSION

The key to unlocking the Bible, the treasure chest of truth, is the Lord Jesus Christ, who is seen from Genesis to Revelation. In John 5:39, our Saviour stated emphatically that the Scriptures stand as a testimony to who He is and what He came to do for all humankind. In the early days of the church, the reading of God's Word was a priority for God's people (1 Timothy 4:13). In the eighth and ninth chapters of Nehemiah, the reading of the law (the books of Moses) took place on a regular basis; the Scriptures were also taught to the people by their spiritual leaders: *"So they read in the book in the law of God distinctly, and gave the sense, and caused them to understand the reading"* (Nehemiah 8:8, KJV).

We should value the Bible as our chief treasure and make it our daily meditation and ongoing delight. The sweet psalmist of Israel loved God's *"commands more than gold, even the purest gold"* (Psalm 119:127, HCSB).

With so many versions of the English Bible available today, it can be a daunting task to determine a choice of translation. Scholar and translator David Stern, who gave us the Complete Jewish Bible, can assist us here:

> First it is a common belief that there is such a thing as a "best" translation of a text from one language to another. I question that. Languages have different words, different syntaxes [arrangement of words and formation

of sentences], different sentence structures, different semantics [the meaning of a word, phrase, or sentence], different cultures out of which they arise and evolve and many other differences; so that translation cannot be a simple, automated process. Moreover, readers differ. Some prefer a simple style with a modest vocabulary, while others respond to a more elegant or complex style with a larger vocabulary. Even the concept of accuracy is reader-dependent—what scholars might consider an accurate translation might fail to accurately communicate to less informed readers. If translators fail to consider who their readers are, aren't the translators responsible for the lack of communication? Clearly some translations are, by all reasonable standards, worse, while others are better. But because readers differ, no one version can be best for all.[272]

It is imperative to find a translation that best resonates with you. Make it a daily habit to search out the riches of the Bible. It is one thing to know the facts of scripture, but quite another to know our Lord in a personal way. God's desire is for us to trust him by faith, enabling us to rightly relate to Him. The words of John 3:16 speak of a loving God who has given all that is necessary for our redemption:

For God so loved the world that He gave His only begotten Son, that whoever believes in Him should not perish but have everlasting life. (NKJV)

We have learned that God has not only made provision for our eternal salvation but has given us His word, which can be safely trusted. His word is preserved in heaven (Psalm 119:89), and to have His word in our language of understanding is undoubtedly our greatest treasure.

He [God] removeth the scales from our eyes… that we may understand His word, enlarging our hearts, yea, correcting our affections, that we may love it above gold and silver, yea that we may love it to the end. Ye are brought unto fountains of living water.[273]

---

[272] David H. Stern, Complete Jewish Bible (Clarksville, MD: Jewish New Testament Publications, 1998), xiv.
[273] *The Bible with the Apocrypha, King James Version* (London, UK: The Folio Society, 2008), xxxv. From "The Translators to the Reader."